101 PRINCIPLES TO WEALTH

Charles Brokop

Clear Wealth Publishing

CW Publishing

Printed in the United States of America

Disclaimer:

All the material contained in this book is provided for educational and informational purposes only. No responsibility can be taken for any results or outcomes resulting from the use of this material.

While every attempt has been made to provide information that is both accurate and effective, the author does not assume any responsibility for the accuracy or use or misuse of this information.

As a registered investment advisor I am not authorized or qualified to give personal tax advice. Any tax information in this book is for education and general purposes. In regard to your specific situation please see your tax advisor or tax professional. Other investment recommendations are for general purposes and should not be taken to apply to your specific situation. Please consult your investment professional when applying to your personal situation. Investing involves risk and you may lose part or all of your principle.

ISBN: 0692212124
ISBN-13: 978-0692212127

DEDICATION

I dedicate this book to my grandparents; (Mayme and Edward), to my mother; (Camille), to my brothers; (Don, Todd, and Bert), and to my two daughters; (Lexi and Camryn

101 Principles to Wealth

CONTENTS

Forward

I have decided to write this book after many requests from clients, friends, and with much encouragement from many of those influential and close to me. Unfortunately I have seen first-hand, so many people struggle with money and finances and face challenges that give them on-going pain throughout their lives. Many people end up being their worst enemies in the matter of money as well; however, they can also break their bad financial habits. I have certainly had many of my own personal experiences as well in which to learn from and share with others. Fortunately I was raised with wisdom and discipline that gave me the foundation along the way to learn the ins and outs of the financial world both personally and professionally. My maternal grandmother was a banker in Chicago. She possessed a keen understanding of the value of money and how to make it work for people. She was the first person to teach me the important principle of compound interest. She was full of wisdom in so many ways and I was lucky and blessed enough to be her grandson. Throughout my business career I have held various positions in sales, management, and business development prior to launching my own investment firm in 2006. I have studied the financial markets as early as high school, studied accounting and finance in college, and statistics in graduate studies.

Additionally, I have read over 30 books in the area of money, finance, and investing. Regardless of the income I earned I learned the discipline to save some of the income and invest it over time. Some of the investments worked out well, several of them did not. You will have the benefit of learning from my experience, judgment and mistakes at a much lower cost than me. Hopefully you will also learn from my successes and make these positives work for you many years ahead into your future.

In writing this book I tried to stay concise on each principle; however, at times I felt like I could have written a book on each principle themselves. Nonetheless each could have been expanded on for sure yet it would have taken away from keeping the principle simple and quickly applicable. My guess is that many principles will apply to you immediately and some may not, but it is my hope that you think about each of these and tailor them to your own situation and make them your own.

Wishing you the best of success on the road to growing your wealth!

ACKNOWLEDGMENTS

I would like to thank the many people that have supported me in the process of writing this book. First my daughters that give me so much love and inspiration. Thank you for supporting me on the late nights and weekends in my office. Thank you to January Jones for sharing all she has learned in writing her many books and for encouraging me to go forward with this project. I would like to thank my great friend Steve Thoeny for his encouragement and feedback over the years on both this project and with Clear Stream Advisors, my investment firm. A big thank you to my editor Michelle for pouring over this text many times and giving her excellent and candid feedback.

Cover by Sierra Kellermeyer

www.skellermeyerdesigns.com

Introduction:

At one time or another we all have heard people say "I want to be rich", I know I have. However, one of the key things that people need to understand is the difference between a "Want" and a "Wish." People often mistake the 2 phrases "I Wish" and "I Want." Let me give you an example. When someone is sitting on the couch looking at someone on TV that is in great shape and says "I want to look like that," but keeps on sitting on the couch eating chips, they really mean they "Wish" they looked like that. However; if they get up off the couch, stop eating the chips (or other unhealthy food) and start to work out, they "Want" to get in shape. It is the same financially. Looking at Donald Trump and saying "I want to be like Donald", but taking no action or doing nothing about it is really a "Wish." If you buy a lottery ticket you "Wish" to get rich. If you work hard, plan, save and invest you "Want" to get rich. If you are willing to apply the principles in this book you "Want" to get rich and you can. If you read the principles and don't apply them you most likely "Wish" to get wealthy, but most likely will not.

With that being said, you should keep money within the context of your overall life. If your focus is solely on creating wealth without keeping it in perspective, it will likely prove less rewarding than you may originally think. Keep your priorities in order as a lesser return on your finances may make sense in exchange for a higher return on other aspects of your life. This book holds time tested principles that have been around for thousands of years and still hold true today. I sincerely hope you follow them, implement them, and achieve your financial goals. This book is written in a way that allows you to use the principle that you need most now and to apply and follow these in your life. You will probably find that you are already doing some of these in your life today or find some may not currently apply to your personal situation. That is ok; however, you may need that principle in the future so it will be good to get exposure to it now. If you can apply a few of these principles every week it will get you closer to achieving your goals and build your financial confidence. These principles should also help you understand money, finance, investing, saving, and planning so you worry less about your financial future and investments while gaining control over financial matters.

Most people have good intentions in taking action but they usually DO NOT have something in place to, "trigger" them to take action. This book will give you the triggers, exercises, and action to implement toward your success. Let's get started!

SECTION 1: PLANNING & MOTIVATION

Secret Principles

1 *"Empty the coins from your purse into your mind and your mind will fill your purse with coins" -Benjamin Franklin*

Ben Franklin is considered one of the smartest men in America's history; therefore it would be wise to listen to his advice. What Ben Franklin is saying in his quote above is to invest in ourselves in the form of education. More specifically he is saying to invest in financial education or in an education that will help you get a well-paying job. This is called making an investment in ourselves. We can do this by going to school for formal education as well as reading books on subject matter that we want to learn. Then we can apply the knowledge to generate money. We should not only invest time to learn from books but also from other people, directly in workshops, seminars, internships, on the job training, and one on one meetings.

I have personally found that taking a successful person out to lunch or coffee and seeking their advice is an inexpensive cost with valuable and applicable life lessons. Most successful people are happy to share their personal success traits and help coach or mentor others. This type of feedback is incredibly valuable as it is usually specific to your personal situation. Also hearing from someone that has been successful will generally allow you to learn from their mistakes and avoid some of the pitfalls that they may have experienced.

Consider the return on investment of any type of education. When you learn something that you can apply in your life you will be able to apply that education or skill for the rest of your life. You may only sacrifice a few hours in reading a book or a year or two in education that pays you back for decades. The fact that you are reading this book is a great start or continuation of your investment in your future.

2 *Create a simple net worth statement every quarter.*

A net worth statement is a numbers calculation of how much you are worth in dollar value. This written statement simply calculates all your assets (money & things you own) then subtracts all your debts (money you owe) and the amount left is your *Net Worth* number. **Net worth** = All Assets minus your Debts. If this number is negative you are in debt and have a negative net worth. You should review and compare your quarterly statements to see the progress you make over quarters and years. This is a very helpful visualization and you can quickly determine if you are making progress and growth. If you are not you should be able to see why not and where potential issue are in your lack of progress. Often debt is a big reason people do not get ahead. If that is the case you may need to find ways to lower your debt or try to consolidate the debt.

I recall the first time I did my own net worth statement early in my career. I had a good job and was making decent money for a college graduate; however, I was surprised to learn that not only was I not worth anything financially I was in debt. It was an eye opener; however, it motivated me to get out of debt and start creating some wealth for myself.

When going on a trip you cannot create the path to your chosen destination without knowing where your starting point is. It is the same with your financial path. You have to know your starting point and then you can determine the course to your destination and also change direction if you get off course. The exercise of determining where you stand financially every quarter will give you the focus of where you are at currently as well as the direction you are presently going. See the form below.

Net Worth Statement

Assets

House	__________
Car	__________
Investment account	__________
Retirement account	__________
Cash Value life insurance	__________
Bank account	__________
Property	__________
Home furnishings	__________
Collectibles	__________
Miscellaneous	__________
Total Assets	__________

Liabilities/Debt

House debt	__________
Car debt	__________
Bank loans	__________

Credit Card 1 __________

Credit Card 2 __________

Miscellaneous __________

Total Debts __________

Total Assets – Total Debts = Net Worth

$ __________

3 *How to think like a millionaire*

Most people believe that millionaires live extremely lavish life styles, are driven to work in limousines, always have the finest clothes, and drink only the finest champagne while eating the best caviar. In reality the contrary lifestyle is more the norm for millionaires. In almost all instances millionaires are very conservative with their personal standard of living. Most are extremely concerned about living well within their means, and are careful not to be frivolous with their money. Their general nature is conservative in spending and in investments. According to the book, "Marketing to the Affluent," by Dr. Thomas Stanley, he has found through his research that millionaires are more likely to invest their money in business ventures rather than yachts and furs and reside in a zip codes not known for it's millionaires. Here are some other interesting statistics from his book:

- The most popular watch in a particular group of millionaires was a Seiko.
- Most consumers of $700 suits had an average income of $25,000, not $100,000 or even a million.
- The majority of millionaires surveyed would rather drink beer than champagne.
- Most millionaires underestimate their total networth and do not have conspicuous symbols of wealth.
- Of the millionaires surveyed the majority continue to work as opposed to living off the interest on their investments.
- The norm is to borrow less than 1% of their networth to buy items other than their personal residence and automobiles.
- They spend less than their annual incomes even though they have very significant savings.

Many of the points above may surprise quite a few people and they should. Some people are shocked that millionaires do not live up to their stereotype. The main points that you should extract from this information is that the conservative lifestyle is part of the reason that they are millionaires and even though they have accumulated vast wealth, they still live within their financial means.

4 *Plans fail for lack of counsel, but with many advisers they succeed.*

-Proverbs 15:22

If you were having a house built and the carpenter just started hammering nails and cutting wood without looking at the plans you would be quite concerned wouldn't you? You would want to know that a plan exists and that an architect had plans approved and has an end goal in mind. The same should be said when planning your financial future. Therefore, I strongly suggest that you start to plan your financial future today. You don't need to get the entire plan done in a day. Getting started is a key element in your progress. Start by writing down where you are today financially and where you would like to be in 5 years, 10 years, and 25 years. It has been said, "if you don't do anything now you may just be in the same place you are today in 5 years." That can be a bit scary and should provide some motivation for you. Successful people use experts in the area of accounting for taxes, financial planners and lawyers to write contracts and legal agreements. If you try to perform tasks yourself that you are not knowledgeable on you may end up costing yourself more time and money in the long run. Consider using experts in specific fields to help you before embarking on projects. You should also get estimates on potential costs so you know and understand the value you will receive for the service prior to implementation. By estimating costs you can decide whether or not the advice or service is going to be commensurate with the expense of the service and worth it to you.

5 *That which is not measured does not get your attention and effort.*

It has been said that, "That which is not measured does not get your attention or focus." Think about going to school knowing that several classes that you take you would be graded. Would you work your hardest to study for a test that you knew you wouldn't get a grade on? Of course not. It is the same in most of the things we do in life. If we know that we don't have an outcome in our work and efforts we are not going to put a lot of effort into the results. So writing your plan and/or goals down and looking at them at least once every three days can have a huge impact on the outcome and results. It will keep you focused on doing the daily tasks that will get you to your end result and help you make small sacrafices along the way toward your goal.

In 1957 Yale University conducted a study of graduating students that had a written plan for their future. They tracked the study for 20 years after the students graduated. The study indicated that 3% of the students graduating had a written plan for their future, the other 97% did not have a written plan. The findings are absolutely amazing. After 20 years the 3% of students that had a written plan had achieved more financially that the other 97% of students combined.

I have personally witnessed the above with many people over decades and it amazes me there seems to be something magical about it. In reality it comes down to small daily steps that help you go a long distance. Just like a marathon runner. If they never start the race or go the wrong direction they will never end up at the finish line. Often the first steps are the toughest but are critical in reaching the finish line.

6 *Write down 5 new ways to make some extra money. Commit to at least 2 of them over the next 2 months.*

Writing ideas down have proven to help people clarify their thinking and focus. When you are writing 5 new ideas about making money, it will help you to brainstorm and come up with some ways to raise more money. Some may even seem crazy at the time. However, you may look back a year later and realize that you actually acted on one of the ideas. I'll help you here a bit in suggesting some ideas like a garage sale, selling some unused items around the house on craigs-list or ebay, a new small business, or even a part-time job a few days per week. I know some people that have taken a hobby in which they enjoy making things and then sell them at weekend fairs. They have fun and make a little extra income along the way.

The exercise here is to get you to change your thinking and also for you to take action on at least 2 of these ideas in 60 days. If they are successful for you the success should motivate you to come up with more ideas and take further action to generate more money for yourself. The key is to generate and tap into your creativity. If you don't start this exercise or try it you will unlikely come up with new ideas to generate additional income. Many people have started successful businesses while inititially thinking of just a small way to make a little extra income. So the possibilities can be much larger than you think.

7 *Think and Plan Ahead*

I have heard it said many times, "no one plans to fail, but many fail to plan." Plan out what you will do with your money before you make it or inherit it. You will make much better decisions before the money is right in front of you. So many people do not think ahead about what they want to do with their money and what type of lifestyle they want to create. So when they start making money they just start spending it on things that they did not give much thought to. Don't get me wrong it is ok to enjoy spending money that you have worked hard for. However, too many people have regrets about spending money and wished later that they had saved for their future. If you think ahead about what you would like to do with a certain amount of money, how you would like to invest it, and see it grow, you should be more easily motivated to stay disciplined in staying with your plan.

Set yourself apart. Plan prior to earning the money and you will be far better off than most people.

Other things can be done in planning ahead as well in life that can save a lot of money.

Try to always think ahead of what you may need when you and your family are away from home. Something simple like packing lunches ahead when on the road are often far less than going out to eat. If you are taking your family out for a long day think about clothing when it gets cooler at night so you don't have to buy expensive sweatshirts, at the amusement park or other outing.

8 Limit your debt on *major purchases*

If you have to purchase major items with debt, (ie. A car, home furnishings, and your home) set a debt limit for yourself and do not exceed it. Paying interest on items that you finance is an extra cost for you. Whenever purchasing an item that is financed don't just think of the price tag, but the amount you will end up paying over the time of the loan. Buying a car for $12,000 and financing it at 8% over 4 years will cost you a total of $14,061 over the 4 years. Now financing is not necessarily bad, but you should understand what it will cost you over time. In the example above interest will cost you over $2,000 or about $500 per year. Also you should try to think in term of lowering your payment so you can take the extra money and invest it in something that will pay you back over time.

Let's compare 2 scenarios. First we will look at the previous example; secondly we will look at an example of buying a car for a lower price of $10,000. We will assume both scenarios are financed at 8% over 4 years but the 2nd cars savings per month are invested in an investment that pays you 8% per year. Look at the chart below and notice the extra money in your pocket at the end of the 4 years.

	Car 1	Car 2
Cost of vehicle	$12,000	$10,000
Montly payment:	$293	$244
Total payments:	$14,061	$11,718
Difference in payments :		$2,343 Less

A $49 per month difference in car payments invested at 8% per year is worth $2,774 after 4 years!

Notice how you are now much better off than just the $2,000 saving initially on the cost of the vehicle? Debt works against you while saving and investing works for you.

9 *Have written goals and images that you want to attain*

Write down your goals for your wealth in terms of the value you would like to achieve in various time periods. You should have 6 month goals, 1 year, 3 year, 5 year, and longer term goals. It is certainly helpful to write down your goals and you need to stay focused on them periodically. Some people I know have put their written goals on their bathroom mirror, refrigerator, or someplace else in their home so they see them every day.

Visualization has proven to be successful and helpful to people in attaining things and changing behavior. For most of us we will have to change behavior to create more wealth. If you visualize the changes you need to make prior to taking action, it will make the changes easier for you when you have to actually do them. Part of the reason is that we subconsciously visualize the end goal in mind when performing tasks that help us get closer to our goal.

I have known people that cut out pictures from magazines of

things they want to attain, or even images of how they want to look, and post those on places in their home that they will see daily. They use these images as motivation to drive them toward the results in the photos. That way they have and end goal and clear picture of what they are shooting for every day, whether it is a new home, new car, or losing weight they can see the target clear and often. Seeing the goal daily should produce a positive feeling in you that makes you take action toward that goal and avoid activity that will keep you from achieving those clearly defined goals.

You may use a combination of written statements and photos that define the type of lifestyle you want. It may be living in a certain type of neighborhood, having a certain type of furniture, or belonging to a high-end fitness club. Images of the day to day living that you want should help you strengthen your resolve daily toward your goals.

10 *Stay healthy!*

Stay healthy and be proactive in taking care of yourself. You have probably heard the saying, "an ounce of prevention is worth a pound of cure." If you exercise regularly, rest, and eat right you will cut back on illnesses which can cost a lot of money in medical bills and lost wages. Studies have shown that by getting regular exercise and plenty of rest your white blood cells are increased which helps you fight off illness by having a stronger resistance. You don't need to spend the money on a gym membership either. Just walking 30-40 minutes per day has been shown to provide benefits and burn calories. You can find a lot of home workouts for free on YouTube as well and there are many workout shows on TV that you may be paying for with your existing television service.

Also eating right is a very helpful in keeping you healthy and increasing your resistance to various viruses. Often the healthier choices on food can be less expensive than processed foods. A simple choice of drinking water when eating out is both healthier and cheaper. When eating healthier you will most likely find that you have more desire to exercise as well. You will also have more energy to exercise if you eat healthy. If you stay healthy you will be able to work more days and be more productive in the process. Lastly if you stay healthy you won't have the cost of going to the doctor's office or urgent care as often which can save you hundreds of dollars per year.

11 *"Increase your income or decrease your*

wants" -Socrates

This simple princple is one of the most important priciples that you may learn in your lifetime and it is over a thousand years old. This saying has certainly stood the test of time. If you can learn to live within your means you will create a tremendous opportunity for yourself. This will not always be easy. However, it will get easier as you get in the habit of not over spending your income. I have said that short-term sacrafices over time will result in long-term gains. Many people struggle to make those simple short-term sacrafices.

Take an athlete for example. If a person wakes up one day and wants to try out for the Olympics without any training and sacrifice most people would laugh at them. Any successful athlete will use the term sacrific. They clearly understand that they have to train to be successful and even train and exercise at times when they do not want to. Lance Armstrong talked about times when he hated training but knew it was necessary to get him the results he wanted.

The definition of sacrifice is to give up something for a better cause or to attain something else. So that is why living within your means and giving up certain things will not always be easy.

12 *Stay ahead of Inflation*

Here is an old joke to illustrate the effects of inflation:

A man has one million dollars and goes to a financial advisor to invest his money. After investing the money the man goes on a cruise and the ship wrecks on a deserted island and the people get stranded for 20 years. After 20 years they are found by another ship. Once they return to civilization the first thing the man does is finds an old pay phone, calls his financial advisor and asks how his investments have done. The financial advisor reply's saying, "I have good news and bad news. The good news is that your investment is now worth $20,000,000. However, the bad news is"…..then there is a pause and the operator comes onto the phone and says, "Sir, please deposit $100,000 for the next 5 minutes."

The key in investing is to stay ahead of inflation and create more purchasing power with your money in the future. If you save money for future expenses and the money you save and invest doesn't grow at the rate of the future price, you have lost ground to inflation or lost purchasing power with your money. This is why putting money under your mattress is not a good idea. You may be able to buy 30 gallons of milk with that money today, but years from now without the money growing, you may only buy 20 gallons of milk. That is money that is not working for you and it cost you 10 gallons of milk over time. In the same line of thinking, your growing assets should be based on the purchasing power of the assets in the future. In the joke above the man is initially excited at the value of his money but he didn't know the full story that everything is much more expensive in the future. If you understand the cost of living now and the direction of the cost of living in the future, this understanding will allow you to save and invest with a clear anticipation of keeping pace with inflation or getting ahead of inflation.

13 *Understand the Costs & Benefits of buying a home*

Buying a home can be very exciting, emotional, and very rewarding. There is a lot of pride in home ownership and also a lot of work. The work is beyond just paying the down payment and mortgage. You will certainly have maintenance on the home from time to time as issues will happen to every home over time. Things from new paint to plumbing problems can happen at unexpected times. You will be rewarded over time in home ownership as long as the home appreciates in value over the period in which you own it. Also, if you do a traditional mortgage part of your monthly payment goes to the principle and part goes to paying interest. The principle is really equity in the home that you get back some day, so you can look at it as paying yourself.

Initially upon purchasing a home you will have closing costs which are about 2 to 4 percent of the purchase price of the home and will generally include title insurance, escrow fees (home owners insurance), credit report, loan origination, and appraisal fees. Most mortgage companies will allow you to put the closing fees into the mortgage loan; however, you will end up paying interest on these costs over time.

You will also need to determine the amount of money you will put toward the down-payment. Generally the minimum you can put down is 3%. If you can put a down-payment of 20 percent of the cost of the home you will not have to pay private mortgage insurance (PMI). PMI can add several hundred dollars to the monthly payment. Private mortgage insurance is insurance that is paid in case you decide not to pay your mortgage.

14 *Various roads to a million*

Not all millionaires took the same path to their millions. Everyone is different and the timing is different as well. I know many people that have sold businesses for several million dollars. What most people don't realize that the people that sold those businesses often said, "No," to many previous offers to buy their businesses. Look at Mark Zuckerberg of Facebook. He had many offers to buy his entire business for millions but he turn the offers down to continue growing the business and is now a billionaire. Individuals can do the same thing with their own personal finances by saying, "no," in spending the money and taking out of investments. Look at the comparisons below and the various lengths of time to reach a million dollars in an account. It often surprises people how soon they can reach that goal, but the key is that they do not spend the princple and let the money grow and work for them. Note: each example on the next page is for illustration purposes and assumes 10% annual growth with the top value added each year and no consideration is given for taxes.

Year	Plan 1	Plan 2	Plan 3
1	$10,000	$25,000	$35,000
2	$21,000	$52,500	$73,500
3	$33,100	$82,750	$115,850
4	$46,410	$116,025	$162,435
5	$61,051	$152,628	$213,679
6	$77,156	$192,890	$270,046
7	$94,872	$237,179	$332,051
8	$114,359	$285,897	$400,256
9	$135,795	$339,487	$475,282
10	$159,374	$398,436	$557,810
11	$185,312	$463,279	$648,591
12	$213,843	$534,607	$748,450
13	$245,227	$613,068	$858,295
14	$279,750	$699,375	$979,124
15	$317,725	$794,312	$1,112,037
16	$359,497	$898,743	
17	$405,447	$1,013,618	
18	$455,992		
19	$511,591		
20	$572,750		
21	$640,025		
22	$714,027		
23	$795,430		
24	$884,973		
25	$983,471		
26	$1,091,818		

15 *Understand the balance of money & labor*

Understand where your money goes in both overall expenses

and in your efforts or labor in your job. See the following charts. Take note of the the various costs in each of these categories. This should help you visualize cutting some expenses along the way when you realize the percentage that you are contributing to each of these cost categories. The 2nd chart shows the amount of time you take in an 8 hour day toward various expenses. This chart is often initially upsetting to people as they realize they are not only working for their own benefit. Notice the amount of hours that you work for yourself in a given day. It is about 5.15 hours per day.

I would suggest that you create your own pie chart of where your money goes as well. You can make a simple hand writen one or get more detailed and sophisicated by creating one in a spreadsheet or in software like Quicken.

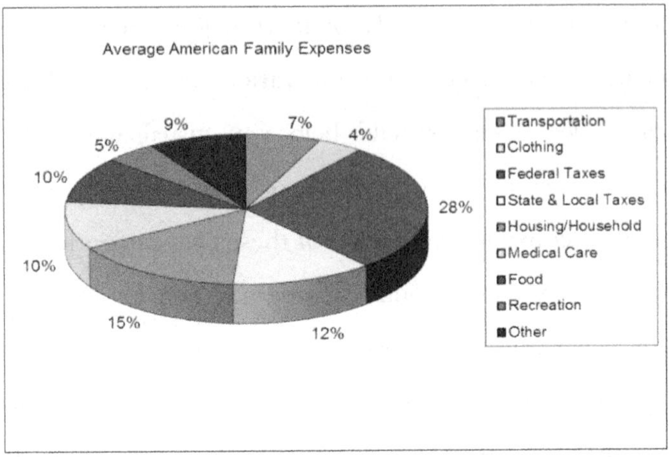

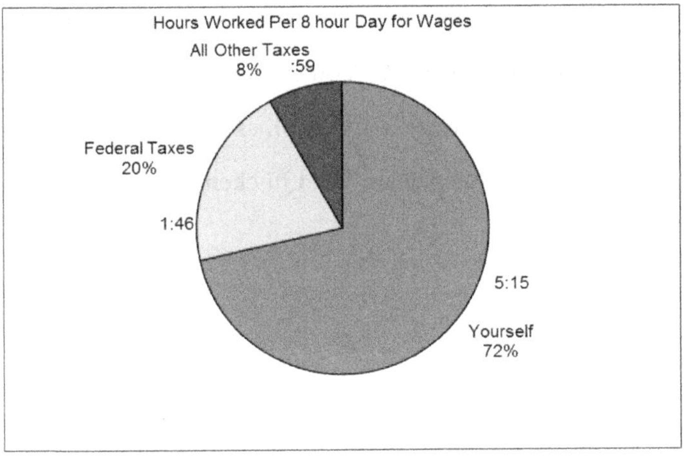

16 *Keep your credit rating high*

Keeping your credit rating high says a lot about someone's responsibility and honor. Businesses want to do business with people that are responsible and honorable. That is why you may have heard it said that banks only give loans to people that don't need loans. The banks as lending agencies want a strong assurance that they will get their money back when loaned out.

In keeping your credit rating high you will be able to get a loan when you need it and at a better rate than someone that has a low credit rating. The best way to get or keep your credit rating high is to pay your obligations on time. If you can't pay them on time call the company that you owe the money to and explain the situation and at least pay something to them in good faith. People that make at least partial payments are less likely to have their credit rating hit. Also don't apply for credit more than once per quarter. If you do apply often it can negatively affect your credit score.

Make sure you check your credit score once a year. It is free on several services online, like Equifax or FreeCreditScore.com. If you have bad marks that are valid, clean them up by paying them down even with partial payments. If you don't agree with the negative mark on your rating, you can write a letter to the agency and dispute the claim, being sure to give specific reasons and include any documents that are helpful. You can also offer to write a letter to a company asking them to take off the complaint on your credit rating if you start to pay off the debt on a monthly basis. Some may work with you in that way as they just want to get paid the amount of debt they are owed from you.

17 *Support the Goose that is laying the Golden Eggs*

I always loved the fable "Jack and the Beanstalk" as a child. You just did not want to let go of that goose that was laying the Golden Eggs. Most fables have a valuable life lesson as does this one. When we have something of value that continues to create more value we should not easily let go of it. For most people their job is that goose that is allowing us to create monetary value. Therefore, we should be grateful for having a job and having an opportunity to generate income. We should also make the most of that opportunity as well in doing the best you can while striving for a raise and/or promotion. You may be at a job that does not have a path for a promotion but it is still in your best interest to do the best you can as the current employer will most likely be a reference for your future employment. When my oldest daughter got her first job as a hostess, I told her to be the best hostess that the restaurant has ever seen. The reason is, you want them to be a good reference but you also you never know who you are going to meet that wants to hire you because they like you and see you working hard. As it turned out the owner sold the restaurant and opened up a new one. Guess who he hired? Yep, he hired my daughter again because he knew she worked hard, showed up on time, and she was trained.

Exercise: Make a list of 3 things you have done that have made money for you. Look at these as geese that are laying golden eggs for you. Think about how you can maximize or improve those 3 things, whether it is a job, selling an old car, or investing in something you know. Now continue to do and support those positive efforts. Then make a list of 3 things that have cost or lost money for you. You guessed it....stop doing or supporting these negative efforts now.

18 *Be consistant*

"Press on. Nothing in the world can take the place of perseverance. Talent will not; nothing is more common than unsuccessful men with talent." - Calvin Coolidge, 13th

President of the United States

I love the quote above having seen people succeed with perseverance and yet have also seen people with plenty of talent that have not been successful in life due to laziness. One of the toughest things for most people is to stay on a course and take continuous action toward their goals. Consistent effort can over-take talent over time. I think that is why people are often surprised by successful people and I have heard them say things like: "That person isn't all that smart; I can't believe that they are so successful." I think most successful people would agree and admit that they don't have all the answers and have much to learn. Most will tell you that when things got tough they did not give up but kept working toward their goal or on their business while keeping their vision in mind.

Therefore you should make a point to work toward your financial goals every week. Do something and take some action every week toward making progress. You may want to set a specific day and time to sit down with a pad and write down what you have accomplished the past week and what you would like to achieve in the week ahead. You will find that you may not accomplish and check off all things in a week but you will start to take action on them. Other small tasks may be as simple as a quick phone call that can end up saving you money for months. The key here is to start to take some action and continue that action once you are in motion.

19 *Review Taxes Prior to year-end*

The worst time to do tax planning is when the year is over and you are filling out your tax forms. Review your taxes at the end of October or early November for the current year. That way you will have a couple of months to make any changes or adjustments necessary that can have an impact on the current years taxes. You should review your current income, any realized tax gains and losses, and any other major life choices like buying a house or having a child. If you can plan ahead you should be able to save some money by making the correct choices before the year end.

Make sure you can benefit and afford to fund your retirement accounts prior to the end of the year, even though you have until April 15th of the next year to put the money into your account. Be sure to try and match up your accounts realized gains and losses, as that can save money on your taxes from the gain on a sale of an asset. If you are going to realize a taxable gain near the end of the year you may want to wait just a couple of months and put it into the next calendar and tax year. That is a method of deferring the taxes for 1 year. Keeping good records throughout the year will be beneficial when it comes time to prepare your taxes as well. A little organization throughout the year will save you hours of digging around trying to find documents and receipts come tax time.

20 *Use online calculators*

When you want to make some quick projections on figures, there are some great free online tools, you can use to get quick answers and figures. If you simply search online for "financial calculators" you will get a lot of resources from which to choose. Most of these have retirement projections and will take your input on how much you have saved, how much you plan to add to your retirement each year, a projected interest rate, and how much time you have. After putting in the numbers you will get an almost immediate figure or projection of your retirement value. This exercise will allow you to change some of the variables which will give you several scenarios to help you look at prior to starting your course to your goals. This will also allow you to see what variables need to change and help you focus on those areas most. For example needing to get a higher return on savings or possibly needing to work a few more years prior to retirement.

Most calculators come with payment tools as well. You can also use the tools to determine your mortgage payment prior to buying a home or refinancing or calculate monthly payments on things like auto loans. There are now many free apps on the smart phones that allow you to do the same calculations at the touch of your fingers.

21 *Anticipate unforeseen expenses*

Most of us like pleasant surprises but none of us like bad unexpected surprises. Unfortunately surprises and emergencies are a part of life. The more you can plan ahead for unforeseen expenses and emergencies the better off you will be and you will be less likely to incur high credit card debt as well. Many people are caught with expenses they did not expect and with no savings on hand to take care of them have to take on debt to pay for the sudden expense.

Set aside some money every month if you can for the unexpected expenses like car trouble, a broken washer, broken vacuum cleaner, or a leaky roof. We should all plan on things wearing out over time. Car tires are a great example of something that gets used almost every day and yet has a useful life to it. If we mentally prepare for things wearing out or breaking we will most likely be better at setting some money aside for these unexpected and unplanned expenses. If you save money for a partial payment toward an unexpected expense, it will help ease the burden a bit and help keep your debt down.

22 *Understand the taxes that you pay*

On a percentage basis taxes are one of our largest costs. Even though the details intimidate many people you should still take the time to understand the framework of taxes because they are most likely your largest lifetime expense. You don't need to understand every detail of the tax code, but you should understand the big ones that affect you. I have heard people say that they heard of someone making more money and they were bumped into a higher tax bracket and actually lost money. That is not accurate as the tax code is a graduated scale, meaning you pay more in taxes on amounts over certain thresholds, you don't pay higher tax on all income. For example you may pay 10% on the first $12,000 earned, then 12% on $12,001 to $15,000, then 15%

on $15,001 to $18,000 and so on. This is just an example and not to be considered tax advice.

Make sure you are taking advantage of any tax deductions or write-offs that you can. These can lower your overall taxable income, so keep a good record of receipts and donations throughout the year. Contributions to 401K's and IRA plans can lower your overall taxable income as well.

Be sure to understand the difference between a *Tax Credit* and *Tax Deduction* as they are different. A tax credit is a dollar for dollar amount off the tax owe after you have almost completed your tax form. A tax deduction is deducted from your adjusted gross income, (AGI) and calculated prior to figuring out the tax owed. For example if you have $50,000 of AGI and you have deductions of $2,500, your taxable income would be $47,500. If you owe $3,000 in taxes and have a tax credit of $300 you tax owed is now $2,700 after the credit.

There is obviously a lot of complication to the tax code so take some time to find out how it applies to you and talk to a tax professional so you don't pay more than your share.

23 *Conquer debt*

Having some debt on your home or even on your automobile at a reasonable interest rate is ok if you can afford it. However, if you are working every month just to keep up with credit cards your debt has a hold of you. Being in debt with high interest payments can just continue to eat away at your ability to save and get ahead. Debt can pile up and soon it is like a runaway train and you don't make enough to pay the monthly payments. The faster you can get focused on getting out of debt on credit cards and any other high interest rate loans, the better off you'll be. If you have a lot of debt at high rates, talk to a debt consolidator to reduce your overall payments and potentially lower the interest rate as well.

One way to do this is to create a list of your debts, other than home, and put that list in a place that you'll see it every day. When you play down some of the debt, cross off the old number and put your new number so you'll see the progress you are making on getting the debt off your books so to speak. I heard someone say "the only way to eat an elephant is one bite at a time." If you see the debt day to day, it should help you spend more carefully and not generate more debt.

Seeing the debt can also keep you working to knocking it off the list.

24 *Take small steps toward your goals*

"The journey of a thousand miles starts with one step"

-Lao Tzu

Looking at a very long-term goal can often be overwhelming as it can seem so far in the distance and so large it appears impossible to attain.

Use short-term tactical actions and activities that propel you toward your goal.

Don't get discouraged at small setbacks as some are bound to happen and you should expect them from time to time. If you let brief bumps along the road to your goals completely upset you it can get you off course and may even stop you from continuing on the path to your goals.

Create weekly and monthly lists of action and tasks that you plan to take toward your goals and check them off when you are completing the activities. This exercise should help you psychologically because you should feel yourself making progress toward your goals. While you may not see a lot of results in the shorter term the activity and accomplishment of tactical tasks should help you see that you are in fact making progress. It is often the very small actions put together in total that help you get to your final goal.

Think of a large brick building for example. It seems over whelming that people put each brick in place by hand and mortared each brick as well. Yet over time brick by brick the entire building goes up and one day it is finished. I'm sure it may have been tough for those first few brick layers to start the process of putting the bricks in place toward the ultimate goal; however, without that first small step the building never gets started, nor completed.

SECTION 2: INVESTING

Secret Principles

25 *Would you rather have $30,000 today or 1 penny on day 1 that doubles every day for 31 days?*

You will find this hard to believe but the 1 penny doubling every day for 31 days ends up totaling: $10,737,418.00 Yes that is correct, over 10 Million Dollars! This is an example of the magic of compounding at work. At the end of 8 days you would have only $1.28. If you were to take out a $1.00 after day 8 and then let the remainder ($0.28) continue to double you would only have about 1/10 of the above figure or $1,174,405. (See the next table) Not bad, but a hefty amount for $1.00 taken out very early in the process. This is only an illustration but this should have a major mental impact on you in both the magic of compound interest and taking money out of savings early in the process. If you can be patient and not uproot the financial tree that you plant you will be richly rewarded over time. This is one of the big reasons the "rich get richer." Once wealth grows to a significant level it can become tough to spend the interest and gains on the principle.

Day 1	$0.01	$0.01	
Day 2	$0.02	$0.02	
Day 3	$0.04	$0.04	
Day 4	$0.08	$0.08	
Day 5	$0.16	$0.16	
Day 6	$0.32	$0.32	
Day 7	$0.64	$0.64	
Day 8	$1.28	**$1.28**	$1.00 taken out
Day 9	$2.56	$0.28	
Day 10	$5.12	$0.56	
Day 11	$10.24	$1.12	
Day 12	$20.48	$2.24	
Day 13	$40.96	$4.48	
Day 14	$81.92	$8.96	
Day 15	$163.84	$17.92	
Day 16	$327.68	$35.84	
Day 17	$655.36	$71.68	
Day 18	$1,310.72	$143.36	
Day 19	$2,621.44	$286.72	
Day 20	$5,242.88	$573.44	
Day 21	$10,485.76	$1,146.88	
Day 22	$20,971.52	$2,293.76	
Day 23	$41,943.04	$4,587.52	
Day 24	$83,886.08	$9,175.04	
Day 25	$167,772.16	$18,350.08	
Day 26	$335,544.32	$36,700.16	
Day 27	$671,088.64	$73,400.32	
Day 28	$1,342,177.28	$146,800.64	
Day 29	$2,684,354.56	$293,601.28	
Day 30	$5,368,709.12	$587,202.56	
Day 31	**$10,737,418.24**	**$1,174,405.12**	

26 *The Rule of 72.*

The Rule of 72 is a method of estimating the amount of time an investment takes to double or the interest rate needed to double an investment in a fixed period of time. To figure out how long it will take to double and investment you simply take the number 72 and divide it by the expected rate of return. For example if you invest some money at 9%, you would take 72 (the rule) divided by 9 (the interest rate) to give you 8 years, as the time period in the above example to double your money. Example 72/9 = 8.

You can also figure out the rate of return on an investment if you know the length of time it will take to double. If you had an investment double over a period of 10 years, you can take 72 and divide it by 10 (number of years) and you get 7.2 which is your rate of return annually. So now you will know that your return was 7.2 percent or your estimated return would be 7.2 over that time period.

This simple formula or method is very helpful in understanding, estimating, and setting expectations on rates of return or calculating the time period to double your money. The benefit of this method is that it is quick and relatively simple and can be done without spreadsheets to give you a fast estimation of figures.

27 *Preserve your capital.*

Warren Buffet has a sign in his office that is called, "The 2 Rules to Investing." Rule #1 is Never Lose Money, Rule # 2 says, See Rule #1. Warren Buffett for those that don't know is a multi-billionaire and is known as one of the greatest investors of all-time, and he also owns Gieco the insurance company. The reason for the above rule is that he understands how difficult it is to make money back that is lost in the first place.

When investing and incurring a loss it is key to understanding the rate of return it takes to recover from a loss. For example if you lose $50, on a $100 investment, you have lost 50%. To gain back that $50; however, you will need to have a $50 gain, which is now a 100% gain, to get back to break-even on your original $100 investment. I assure you 100% gains are not easy to come by, so you will need to consider the loss of time as well that it will take in the process of recoverying lost capital.

Be conservative and realistic on the return you will make on investments. History shows that long-term investments make around 6%-10% as a guide line. It is difficult to make much more over long periods of time for most people.

Also understand that when you lose the following percentage

you will have to have a larger gain to get back to your original investment amount.

See the table below:

Amount of loss	Gain or return need to get back to even
10%	12.5%
20%	25%
50%	100%
80%	400%

It is easily forgotten just how difficult it can be to make up lost ground or lost capital. That is why most successful investors think about capital preservation first.

Some people are so determined to preserve capital that they keep their money under their mattress. That is not wise either and not the definition of preservation of capital because you will lose purchasing power over time due to inflation. A strong example of this is that money under a mattress does not return any interest or gains over time. If inflation is 5% per year after 14 years the money under a mattress would only have half the purchasing power it did 14 years prior. That is why investing to keep pace with inflation is important and better to get returns above inflation rates.

28 *Diversify your investments.*

This is a defensive strategy so that you don't put all your eggs in one basket. If you have all your savings in one investment, and that investment goes bad, you can lose a large portion or everything in a hurry. By owning various asset classes: Stocks, Bonds, Real Estate, International Funds, US Funds, and Energy Funds, you mitigate your risk. For example, if you have 20% of your assets in stocks and those stocks lose 25%, your entire asset value will only go down 5% if all other assets don't change. Let's clarify showing you the math. If your stocks are valued at $20,000, 25% of that is $5,000. The $5,000 is only part (5%) of your overall $100,000 value (100%) of all your assest.

You should be aware that one can over-diversify when investing. This happens when investing in different looking invsestments that are the same or very similar, which can give you the illusion of diversification without the benefits. You can lower your returns due to added expenses, trading costs, as well as off-setting investments. Also if you are simply diversified in assets that go in opposite directions during certain market movements you can be subjected to the see-saw effect and not see overall asset growth.

Lastly, when investing in stocks, companies, or funds, diversify not only in different stocks and funds, but in different industries and market sectors that have unrelated businesses. For example don't buy a retail company and a shipping company expecting them to perform differently. They will both be impacted in an economic slowdown. Try buying companies in the service industry that have strong recurring revenue regardless of market slow-downs. The energy industry is a good example of this as people will still need to drive and use electricity in a slow economy.

29 *Lazy hands make for poverty, but diligent hands bring wealth. -Proverbs 10:4*

This was probably recorded about 2500 years ago. This was great wisdom then and is certainly great wisdom now. We all get tired from time to time but we have to fight through those tired feelings and will often get our second wind. This principle applies to not only working hard but working smart as well. That is why the above quote says, "Diligent hands bring wealth." I found this definition of diligence: constant and earnest effort to accomplish what is undertaken; persistent exertion of body or mind.

Think about trying to just give 10 percent more over the next year in your work, in your education of money, and in watching over your money more carefully. I'll bet that your overall return is greater than 10 percent at the end of that one year. It has been said that successful people do what they need to do even though they often don't want to do it. Doing what you need to do to reach your goals will help you overcome the feelings of delay or the harmful results of procrastination.

30 *Start an investment plan now, no matter how small.*

The earlier in your life that you start investing, the more time you allow for compounding interest. Look at the example on the next page regarding an early start to investing. Assuming each person had invested in the same type of account earning 10% interest compounded annually, which person accumulated the most wealth at age 65? Surprising, but it is the one that started earliest but invested the least amount of money.

Person 1: @ Age 26 Invested $2,000 Per Year Until Age 65 In IRA

Total Invested Over 40 Years, $80,000

Value $893,704 @ 65 years of age

Person 2: @ Age 19 Invested $2,000 Per Year Until Age 26

Total Invested Over 7 Years, $14,000

Value $930,641 @ 65 years of age

Person 3: @ Age 8 Invested only $6,750 total in small increments to Age 13

Total Invested Over 5 Years, $6,750

Value $1,266,170 @ 65 years of age

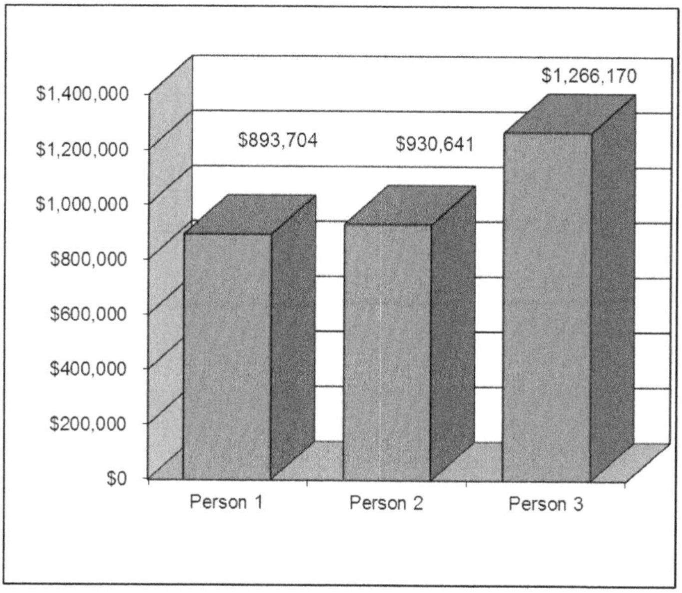

Look at this chart, a picture tells a thousand words as they say. Are you surprised? In this case the picture tells over a million dollars. Person 3, with a much smaller initial investment used time on their side to amass a fortune over a great time period. Note in the example above how 3 elements, time, compound interest, initial, and continuing contributions, contributed to each persons varing success. So the key point is to start saving now and contribute at every chance you get.

31 *Start a Roth IRA if you are under 60 years old. It will grow tax- free and when you withdraw the funds they are not taxed.*

A Roth IRA is a unique investment vehicle in that it has special privilages that other investment do not participate in. The key benefits are that the investment can grow untaxed and you do not pay taxes upon withdrawing the funds. You do; however, pay tax on the money prior to putting it into the Roth IRA. You don't need to be an expert on these to make them work for you. You do need to be able to get on the internet and look at various online brokers and complete some simple paperwork to get it set up and then you can deposit funds into your account to get it started. There are limits to the amount you can put into a Roth IRA every year and it does vary by year and also by your age. Do to the continually changing tax laws and variations I will not put exact figures in this section of the book. Keep in mind the above principles of compounding interest and how important the tax-free growth is to you over time. The interest made on a regular account is taxed every year that trims your gains and also the power of compounding in your favor. That is the compelling reason for Roth gains working for you year after year and then taken out without paying income taxes as well.

32 *Start a regular IRA if under 60 years of age and grow your gains tax-deferred.*

A regular IRA allows you to put in money it before paying taxes in the tax year that you put the money into your account. Any gains over time are not taxed until you take the gains out after age 59 ½ years old. That is called tax deferral. If you take money out prior to age 59 ½ you are charged a 10% penalty on the withdrawn money. The current law requires that you make a required minimum distribution after age 72 ½ years old. The distributions are calculated on the amount of your IRA and your life expectancy. There are limits to the amount you can put into your IRA every year. Do to the continually changing tax laws and variations I will not put exact figures in this section of the book. If you invest $2,000 a year into an IRA with 8% per year average returns, after 30 years it would be worth about $227,000. If you invest $2,000 per year with 8% returns per year it would be worth $518,000 after 40 years. Now tax laws may change and probably will by the time you start withdrawing your money, but most people don't take out enough to be in a higher tax bracket so the deferred tax investment is well worth it.

33 *Rule of Thumb- I do not recommend using life insurance products as saving vehicles.*

A life insurance policy was designed to provide funds to family members in the unlikely event of an early death and in that event the primary income earner cannot provide any longer for their family. The design being similar to your car insurance. You pay an amount monthly or quarterly and if you total your car you do not have to buy a new car, the insurance company will give you money in the amount of the value of the car. In the life insurance senario, if you hold the insurance and you die the policy pays an amount to your spouse and/or family to provide for their future. If you decide not to use the policy after paying into it over a period of years it will have a "cash value." The cash value is the amount that you can take out of the policy while you are alive if you choose to cancel the policy. Some policies are sold with an investment benefit and life benefit, however, these are more expensive in your monthly payments and the investment portion has historically been lower than market rates of return. These financial products also are the highest commission product that I have seen. Also you generally don't have flexibility to pull your money out of the investment portion without paying a penalty and paying a high rate of tax on any gains. That is why I have found just buying life insurance for its original intended purpose is generally best. Every situation is different so please consult your investment advisor prior to purchasing and make sure you understand the product prior to purchase.

34 *Do not follow "hot stock tips." Many people lose money trying to make too much. Have realistic expectations.*

People often have good intentions on hearing something exciting about a company and think it may be a good investment or speculation and pass that limited information on to others. The challenge is that people do not understand the entire story and can do more harm than good. When I worked for Cisco Systems I would hear rumors about a company and someone would say, "buy stock in xyz-company because Cisco is looking at buying them." That statement may have been true; however, the major challenge was that large companies like Cisco Systems or Microsoft are generally looking at hundreds of companies at once and do not buy most of the companies they look at buying. The rumors can often push up the price of the stock when many speculators buy into the stock, then when they realize a takeover will not happen, the stock then drops and many lose money. I have even seen takeovers happen but the stock drops because the price is not a premium to the stock. That can certainly send a shock to the speculators.

"I've learned that when a man with money meets a man with experience, the man with the experience ends up with the money and the man with the money ends up with the experience."

35 *When Investing small amounts buy mutual funds*

When starting out in investing without substantial assets or money I recommend investing in a mutual fund or a couple of mutual funds to start. A mutual fund is a company that pools investor's money and buys various stocks in a variety of companies in different industries. The investor benefits in being in a fund because the fund owns more stocks than an individual investor could possilby buy on their own for a couple thousand dollars. The individual investor has one transaction cost in buying the mutual fund while they could possibly have hundreds of trades in buying individual stocks.

A mutual fund also gives you diversification in owning a vast array of stocks that would not be possible with smaller amounts of money. I usually put the level at under $5,000 of investable money when deciding whether or not to buy mutual funds or stocks.

When looking for mutual funds to invest in look at funds that have a solid long-term track records of 5 or 10 years if possible. Do not just look at the past year or two of performance whether good or bad as that is too short a track record when investing for the long-term. Also look at all the fees of the fund and try to buy no-load funds. Load funds charge a fairly large fee just for buying in and that gives you less money working for you upon initial investment. You should decide on the type of fund by looking at more than just the name of the fund as well. For example a fund may be called a "Dividend Real Estate Fund," but when you look at the prospectus showing stocks held by the fund it may not have many stock holdings in real estate that pay dividends. Look at the prospectus to make sure you know what you are buying.

Lastly you should know whether it is a Open End Fund or a Closed End Fund. An Open End Fund is always open to new investors and can only be bought and priced at the end of the day based on the Net Asset Value (NAV). A Closed

End Fund takes a limited amount of money from investors upon initially opening the fund, then stops at a determined threshold. It then invests that money and has shareholders. The shareholders, of which you can become one, can buy or sell the shares of the closed end fund during the day like a stock. The benefit with the closed-end fund is that the fund operators do not have to invest more money just because new investors want to buy into it.

36 *Understand that buying stock represents ownership in a business.*

Quite often people get excited about a company and will buy the stock of that company. We need to remember that a great company does not necessarily mean it will be a great stock to own. When you buy a share or shares of stock in a company you need to understand what you are buying. You should know how many shares are outstanding in a company. That means how many shares offered by the company and owned by people or entities. The price of the stock multiplied by the number of shares outstanding will give you the market capitalization of the company. That is the entire price or market value of the company if you wanted to buy the entire company on that given day. For example a company with a stock price of $50 per share and 2 million shares outstanding would give you a market capitalization of $100,000,000. The calculation is $50 X 2,000,000= $100,000,000

Next you should understand the annual revenue of the company. That is the total dollar volume the company sells over a 1 year period. After that you should find out if the company has any earnings, that is the money the company makes after all expenses. The earnings can be kept by the company or given to shareholders in the form of dividends. You may have heard of a price earnings multiple or P/E ratio. This is a number that is given to the price of the stock divided by the earnings per share of the company. Let's say the company above has $4.00 per share of earnings per year. That company would have a 12.5 Price/Earnings ratio. Calculated as $50/$4.00= 12.5

One way to think about this in a clear headed way is this: Would you part with a $50 dollar bill if you knew someone would give you $4.00 in return for the year? You may get your $50 back, you may get more if the stock appreciates but you could get less in the future if the stock depreciates.

You also will need to project, as you cannot be certain, the future earnings for the company and if the earnings will appear to grow in the future. Someone once asked me about buying a stock in a company that they liked that was selling for about $80 per share. I knew the company had just earned $0.05 per share that year and that is was estimated that the company would earn $0.07 the year after. So I asked the person if they would give me $80 dollars today knowing that I would give them a nickle at the end of the year and then about 7 cents they year after and perhaps 9 cents the third year. They looked at me like I was crazy and said "heck no." I asked them why in the heck would they buy stock in that company then. The light bulb immediately went off with them.

Do not get personally attached to stock you own. The purpose in owning stock in a company is to give you a resonable rate of return on your money.

37 *Look at your personal finances as if you were running a business. "Would you or others invest in You?"*

When investing in a company I always try to look at how responsible the leaders of the company are with the money the company has. If leaders of a company do not exercise good judgement and discipline with the companies money (Really the shareholders money in this case), they will probably not be successful in the long run and I would rather not invest with them. When a company states that they have made money or earnings, they are refering to the money that they get after paying all their bills. So revenue is all the money the company has brought in via their sales. When all the costs and expenses are subtracted from the revenue you get the earnings number. You should think of your personal financial situation along the same line. The amount of money you make at a job every month is not really earnings, but your revenue. The amount of money you get to keep and invest after all your bills is really your earnings. If you are responsible with your money in saving more than you earn, paying your bills on time, and not having much debt, than you are probably close to being positioned like a solid business. If you are spending more than you are making every month, paying bills late, and have significant debt, you have to be honest with yourself. You would not be a business that someone else would want to invest in. In either case try to start running your personal finances as if you were running a business that you wanted others to invest in. If you can honestly say that you would be a good business that has a solid growing future than you are on your way to success.

38 *Understand the psycology of the stock market.*

It has often been said that the stock market *"slides down a slope of hope"* and *"climbs a wall of worry"*. This means the stock market often does the opposite of what is commonly believed to happen by investors. When investor perception becomes more bearish, then it is likely the time to buy or at least close to a buying point. When so many people become bullish, thinking the market cannot go down, it is generally a time to start worrying that the market is over-priced. Warren Buffet has said this about investing, "Be fearful when others are greedy and greedy when others are fearful." That is a generalization, of course, but it seems to work pretty well on various time frames. If you are looking for an easy and logical place to make money, then stock investing is probably not for you. We all hear about the success stories from time to time, but it is not even easy for the professionals to make money in the stock market year after year. It is often difficult for the experts to understand financial statements from companies and some companies have been known to manipulate their statements making it difficult to find certain disclosures. Enron is one example of a company mis-reporting their numbers. Many analysts would have called Enron a 'Blue Chip' company. It was nothing close to that in reality as the company's financial statements did not give an accurate reporting of earnings and cash. (A Blue Chip company is one that has long track record of solid and steady revenue and earnings.)

39 *"Compound interest is the eight wonder of the world." - Albert Einstein*

Compounding is when money you have invested earns a return, and then the next year the earned money makes a return for you as well. It can work for you if you save and invest money. Compounding can also work against you when you have debt balances that you cannot pay off and the interest just continues to grow against you.

Here is a way to look at compound interest verses simple interest. If you were to invest $10,000 at 10% simple interest, you would simply earn $1,000 per year every year. With compound interest you would earn $1,000 the 1st year, then $1,100 the 2nd year, then $1,210 the 3rd year….. each dollar that you earn in interest will earn interest for you the next year. The interest continues to grow like a snowball. It looks like this illustrated below.

\$10,000 X 10% = \$1,000 then added to \$10,000

\$11,000 X 10% = \$1,100 then added to \$11,000

\$12,100 X 10% = \$1,210 then added to \$12,100

\$13,310 X 10% = \$1,331 then added to \$13,310

\$14,641 X 10% = \$1,464 then added to \$14,641

\$16,105 ……

You can see it starts to grow in a hurry. That is why Albert Einstein called compound interest the 8th wonder of the world. If you can understand this concept and use it to your advantage it will be very powerful for you.

"Ten thousand dollars left to earn interest at 8% a year will grow to \$44 Billion in 200 hundred years, but the first hundred years are the hardest."

- Sidney Homer

40 *Invest in areas that you have knowledge in and understand.*

If you don't know anything about collectable cars you should probably stay away from investing in them. I heard a story recently that someone bought a very expensive car and they were told that it was an original; however, they later found out through experts that many things in the car were not original lowering the value of the car significantly. Therefore invest in assets, businesses, and stocks that you know and understand. Avoiding areas and business that you do not understand. This may save you a lot of money by avoiding potential mistakes. In the book "One up on Wall Street," famous investor Peter Lynch talks about the benefit that individuals have in investing in industries and businesses in which they have had personal experience. Having personal experiences as a customer in a particular business can give you a deeper understanding and confidence of how a business actually creates value and ultimately makes money. A deeper knowledge can also help you avoid certain companies or industries that you may see promoted in the media and yet know that internally they are struggling. When working for Cisco Systems I recall seeing our stock getting sold off by investors because of a competitor's poor earnings announcement. Analysts assumed that the entire industry was not doing well; however, I knew that Cisco was taking market share from the competitor and doing very well. Time proved that it was a temporary sell-off and Cisco recovered very well.

You may have been a customer of a company and watched the lines forming out the door or seeing huge lines at the cash register every time you are in that particular store. If that is the case you may want to look into buying the company's stock. Keep in mind you will need to do some due diligence on the value of the business and stock, you can't just assume the stock will do well because the company is busy.

41 *Create different categories for your money.*

Mentally differentiate between the money you spend and the money you invest. For example, create 2 different categories for your dollars, like Green-dollars vs. Red-dollars. The Green-dollars are ones you invest or get a return on, or are used to pay for an appreciating asset like your home. The Red-dollars are consumable dollars that you will never get a return on. Red-dollars are spent not invested, on things like groceries, gas for your car, clothes that depreciate over time, home appliances, and house wares. Too often I have heard people say that they made a good investment, when in reality all they did was spend money. Now there are times that you need to spend money to create value or spend money on an opportunity such as interviewing for a job. Buying a suit for an interview or putting gas into your car to get to the interview can be money well spent. Understand that it is not an investment per say but spending money on an opportunity is just like a company spending money on advertising. This Red/Green dollar exercise will help you clarify categorically where your money is truly flowing and being "invested" or "spent.".

42 *Do not chase past performance.*

"A Wall Street guru: Someone with a high degree of self-delusion and a strong bull market"

- John Kenneth Galbraith

Most investors look at a very short period (past year) of performance and buy into the recent top-performing mutual funds. You may think that they did very well in their returns, but studies have shown that this method of short-term thinking has not been very successful at all. Morningstar was commissioned years ago by Zweig Mutual Funds to study how well investors did in investing in top-performing growth stock funds. The findings showed a group of 219 funds that had earned an average of 12.5% annually over a five-year period; however, those who invested in the funds actually did much worse suffering losses of 2.2% annually on average over the same period.

Why you ask, could the individuals do so poorly? Because small investors typically jump on the bandwagon after a fund has already made a big move up and then jump out when the market is down. Not only do they lose out on the gains but they take most of the loses.

So when looking at a funds performance look at a 5-year or 10-year period of historic returns to get a long term view. Then be patient and try to add to the fund when it is down in price if possible. Your patience and long-term view will be greatly rewarded.

43 *Key Questions to ask before you invest a dime in anything*

- How much risk am I taking with my capital? Can I lose it all or even more than I invest?
- When can I get my money back if I need it?
- What does the company do with the money that I have invested? Do I own part of the company or is it a loan?

- Do I have to pay a fee to invest? Are there any commission or charges that I pay on my investment? If so, what percentage of my capital is going to fees?
- How safe is my capital, is it insured? Is my investment secured by an asset?
- What are the tax consequences on the investment? Is it tax free, tax deferred, or long term capital gains?
- Are there any penalties assessed against my investment if I want to withdraw my money at anytime or early?
- How does the value of my investment increase? Is it through interest, capital appreciation or a combination of the two?
- Is the firm or company I am investing with or through reputable? Is my investment safe-guarded with them? Can the money be stolen?

44 *Continue your financial education*

Read 2 books per year on investing or money management to get new ideas and learn more about investing from other people that have been successful in this endeavor. Consider the vast education that Doctors undergo prior to becoming practicing doctors. They have legal requirements to take a minimum number of continuing education classes per year. In most states they are required to take about 40 hours of continuing education every year. Although doctors are already well educated and may have practiced medicine for years they are required to continue to educate themselves to learn more about medical practices, changes, and new developments in medicine. Certified Financial Planners are also required to have a minimum of 30 hours every 2 years in continuing education to meet the requirements and keep their CFP certification. This continuing education helps them stay current on changes in various financial products and helps them dive deeper into topics that they may not have as much knowledge in.

Therefore even though you may have some education and knowledge in financial matters you should continue to educate yourself in various areas of personal finance and investing. You should choose topics that interest you and that can help you reach your goals faster. As stated above it will allow you to dive deeper into a topic and understand it more clearly in regard to your personal financial situation. Continuing education is important in every high level profession and you should take it equally as seriously when relating it to your personal finances as it affects so many aspects your life.

45 *Understand risk*

Fully understand the risks prior to any investment. The statement in investment documents, "You can lose all or part of your money," as the disclosure says is real. Be prepared for that. I have looked at hundreds of investments, business plans, and presentations over time and not one of them showed a downward slope at any point in the future showing that they would lose money or go out of business. Most people get emotionally tied to their company and excited about the opportunity ahead. It is certainly good to be enthusiastic about a company or business that you start but people are often overly optimistic and not realistic on the amount of time and effort required to educate potential customers and then acquire those customers. Take your time prior to investing and don't get rushed by unnatural deadlines that force you to make quick decisions. Those situations generally do not end well.

The way sophisticated investors look at risk is to look at "Return Of Capital" first and then "Return ON Capital."

"Return of Capital" is the return of the money you invested

or your principle. "The Return on Capital" is the additional money you make from the money you have invested. Getting your initial money returned is most important as I have pointed out in the planning section. When you lose money you lose both stored labor and time and you have to make larger gains in the future to replace the initial value of the principle.

Always ask the tough questions prior to investing such as:

- Is my money insured?
- How will my money be used by the company?
- How will I get my money (principle) back and how long will it take?
- How will I get a return on my money?
- Can I get my money back early if I want it back?
- Can I lose more than I invested?

46 *It pays dividends to invest in companies that pay dividends*

A dividend is a payment that a company or fund makes to the shareholders generally out of the profits or earnings of the company. Dividend payments are generally paid every quarter; however, many companies have now started paying monthly. If a stock claims to have an 8% dividend with the stock priced at $12 per share, they would pay $0.96 per year/ per share. If you owned 100 shares or $1,200 of the stock you would get annual dividend payments of $96 paid to you.

You can do what you want with the dividend payment, spend it, or reinvest it in the company that paid you or into another company. Dividends are currently taxed at a lower rate than most income taxes; however, that may change in the future.

Investing in a company, stock, or fund that pays a dividend is usually a good idea because companies don't pay dividends unless they plan on making money consistently. If a company is not earning money they certainly cannot afford to pay a dividend. Or if a company does not have consistent earnings they will often elect to not pay a dividend. The other reason that companies do not pay dividends is that they elect to put the earnings back into the company to grow, which may be the best use of their capital.

When a company declares a dividend payment it means that the board members have discussed the various options of what is the best use of the company's capital. The board members will also consider whether the company can earn and continue to earn enough money to pay dividends into the foreseeable future. If they vote to pay a dividend, that is a vote of confidence in the earnings power of the company or funds future.

Dividends, over time, can make up for lost ground on the price of a stock. as For example a stock that pays a dividend of 10% per year over 3 years is 30% in dividends. If you have a loss of 10% on the stock over the 3 year period you would still be ahead by 20% over that 3 year investment period.

Lastly over the last 80 years, dividends have accounted for more than 40% of the total return on equities. Dividend stocks and funds are also historically less volatile than non-dividend stocks.

47 *Don't fight the trend*

"He who doesn't fight, but turns and runs, lives to fight another day" Anonymous

Do not fight the overall trend of the market. Historically the markets gets into long-term trends and stays that way for multi-year periods. If you can go with the general trend you will be far better off than trying to go against the grain. This is a general principle with everything from sanding wood or swimming with the current. If you want go in the same direction as the majority movement it will be much easier to make progress by joining along in the same direction as the major movement. If you don't want to go in the direction of the major movement, by at least getting out of the way of the major movement you will not lose any progress.

It is the same in the stock market as the market is a market of stocks. Statistically 86% of all stocks go in the same long-term direction of the overall stock market. Therefore being in a stock or stocks when the market it trending upward will give you a much higher probability of success than trying to fight the trend. The same would be said if the stock market is trending down, it would be a good idea to be out of most of your stock holdings to stay safe and preserve your capital. A good long-term indicator is the 200 day moving average of the S&P500. Above the S&P500 200 day average price is generally a positive sign and below the average is a weaker sign.

You have probably heard the saying, "Don't fight the Fed." That means if the Federal Reserve is tightening money with rising interests rates the market will probably go down or at least have a tough time going up. If the Federal Reserve is loosening money or monetary policy by lowering interest rates the markets generally go up.

48 *Use company 401K plans*

The 401K plans or accounts are one of the most beneficial accounts available for retirement especially when companies offer matching contributions. The only problem is not everyone has access to opening this type of account because not all companies offer them. If your company offers any kind of matching contribution to your savings you should, at a minimum, commit the amount that the company matches as that is free money to you until it come out as you will have to pay taxes on it them. Over time, invested properly with compounding, the matched funds can add substantial value to your account.

Different companies offer variations of the 401K program as well. For example, some companies will contribute 50 cents or 25 cents for every dollar you contribute to your fund. Some will offer a dollar for dollar matching up to several thousand dollars with a limit.

The way the 401K plan works is that funds are deducted before taxes from your paycheck and deposited into your account. You do not pay taxes on the amount deducted from your paycheck until the time of withdraw in retirement. In addition, you earn deferred interest on your account as well. The benefits of the 401K plan over an IRA are several. For starters, you can contribute more to a 401K than an IRA currently, which lowers your taxable income in the year in which you contribute. Another benefit is that once you sign up it is a forced savings plan automatically taken out of your paycheck. It is also easier to take a loan against your 401K plan than an IRA for hardship reasons.

There are penalties for early withdraws in a 401K like an IRA. Specific rules apply to 401K plans on contribution limits, matching contributions, investments availability, and loans. Therefore prior to taking action talk with your plan administrator and your accountant regarding your particular situation.

49 *Understand the bond you have when buying Bonds*

There is a common misconception that there is no risk in bonds, but that is incorrect. There are various types of bonds and some carry more risks than others. With corporate bonds the bond holders stand in the front of the line ahead of common shareholders in getting paid back by the company. If the company ends up going bankrupt the bond holders would get paid prior to any money going to people that hold common stock, but there is still risk that the bond holders do not get paid back everything. If interest rates go up more than the rate the bond pays, the face value of the bond will be discounted on the open market. For example a bond paying 3% with a face value of $100 might only sell for $90 in the open market if new bonds are paying 5% interest.

Bond prices do fluctuate and can have expensive charges or commission to buy or sell them. Most bonds have a maturity date and if you hold the bond to maturity you will get paid the face value of the bond.

Many, but not all, Municiple Bonds are free from state and Federal taxes which make them attractive to people wanting to lower their tax basis. The Muni-bonds carry a lower interest rate but because it is tax-free a lower rate would be equivolent to a higher rate that is taxed. For example if you are in the 35% tax braket a tax free rate of 5% would be like a pre-tax interest rate of 7.7%. In the end you will end up with the same amount of money after taxes. Some bonds are **revenue bonds**, meaning you get paid only if the entitiy creates revenue to pay the bond holders. If they do not generate revenue the bond holders do not get paid, hence there is risk in owning revenue bonds.

Understand the type of bond you are buying prior to buying and the costs. If you are not sure it is best to leave the bond buying to professionals and you can always buy a bond mutual fund.

50 *Collectibles as an investment*

Good luck!

Ok, I guess I should say more on this matter. It seems that the people that really make money in this area are already very wealthy and have intimate knowledge and passion in the area in which they are collecting. The other area people make money is not realizing they have something that is incredibly valueable and perhaps found it in the attic of the home they bought 15 years ago. "Say, what's this old violin doing up here?" Yes it has happened, and the dusted off violin is worth 5 million dollars.

Needless to say people like to collect things and coins are a common one. Try to only collect things that you have a stong interest and knowledge as your chance of a solid return on investment is much higher. You should also really enjoy whatever it is that you are collecting, because in the unlikely event that the collection is not worth much you will at least have a love for the art or whatever else you own.

Collectibles generally carry a wide spread on the buy side verses sell side, that is a nice way of saying that they have very high sales commissions which factors into the value when selling. They can certainly be higher than 10% of the asset value.

If you are still convinced that you should own some collectibles have them insured in case of loss or destruction. You wouldn't want to invest a lot of hard earned money and have it lost in a fire, stolen, or damaged by water. Get a professional appraisal on the collectibles as well as it will help you when selling and also in an insurance claim if needed.

51 *Limit high-risk ventures*

I have looked at hundreds of business plans over the years and not one shows a downward sloping line or a spreadsheet that ultimately ends up out of business. Therefore limit the amount of capital that you invest in high risk ventures like new start-up business or private equity ventures. No matter how good they sound, or how well thought out the business plan looks a lot of new companies fail. The restaurant business is at the very top of the list in terms of failed businesses.

If you are still interested in investing in a high risk venture you should certainly not invests a large portion of your savings into it. Strongly consider the scenario of losing your entire investment after 18 months of investing, and think through how tough that would be. If it will change your lifestyle then do not invest.

Also ask yourself and the business the following questions:

- Does the person or do the people have successful experience in business prior to this?
- Do the person(s) have experience in this exact business?
- Do they have their own money invested as well?
- Do they have other investors that have experience in this industry?
- Do they understand their competition? If they say that they don't have any competition, they don't understand business because every business has competition.
- Are they raising enough money to survive for years with a slow start? Most businesses under estimate

how much money they will need and how long it will take to successfully get the busines running.

52 *Be patient*

Be patient when investing as it can take years to see the results. The early years are often the toughest. It may take years to see tremendous results; however, you will see them if you stick with a plan. Investing is like planting seeds; you will need to keep watering, fertilizing, and weeding around them, then over time your plants will grow and spread their own seeds.

Most investments look like the following graph. Notice how it starts out very slowly in the early years but then really gets momentum and just takes off. In the example below it is assumed that $1,000 is invested initially with with $500 added per year with 8% growth every year. Look at years 1 thru 9 as they are slow and steady but in year 10 it really starts to take off and in year 21 starts to go at higher than a 45 degree angle in growth!

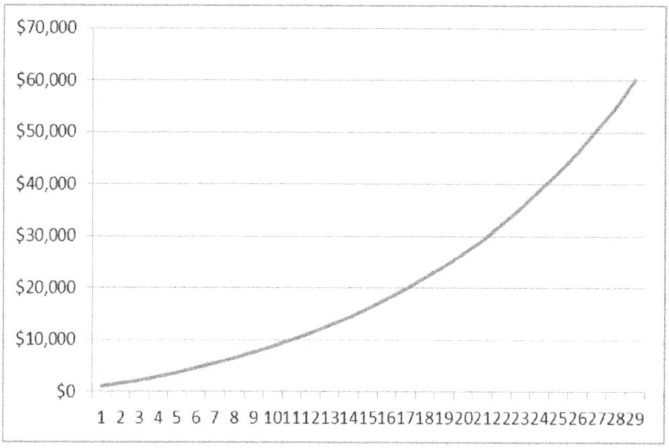

53 *Utilize online tools*

Use online calculators to get quick views on financial situations. By using these you can see how much you need to save annually for retirement and get various views using different rates of return along with different time-frames for retirement dates. You can also run scenarios for your auto payments, mortgages, and student loans. You can put in the assumed or estimated interest rate and amount that you will finance giving you the monthly payment. There are also apps for smart phones that allow you to do these calculations for free at your fingertips. They should be used only as guidelines as interest rates are always changing and other fees can often apply to loans. This is certainly true with a home mortgage.

You should also use online banking and bill paying which should make money management easier to track. You will get daily views if you need them to account balances and your credit card charges as well. With online bill paying you can pay the bills exactly when due which allows you to hold the money a bit longer and with the transaction being electronic you will save money on stamps and envelopes also. The online bank tools can allow you to transfer instantly between accounts as well. Using the online tools should save you a few trips to the bank which is costly in both gas and time.

54 *Finance carefully*

A basic rule of thumb in investing is to pay cash for depreciating assets and finance appreciating assets. Historically this implies financing your home, land, building, or business while paying cash for most other items. Depreciating assets are things that lose value over time and wear out. Automobiles fall into this category, unless they are collectible cars, as well as most of the things we purchase.

As I state above this is a general rule and general rules do not fit every situation. I think young couples starting out in life often need to finance an automobile to get to work every day and transport their family. Interest rate levels should also be taken into consideration when financing a purchase. If you can get a very favorable interest rate and invest the excess capital safely at a higher rate of interest you may want to take advantage of low rates of interest and finance. The challenge is balancing and not taking on too much debt and being conservative on the low risk or risk free rate of return that you can get on your capital. The other issue many people run into is that they finance a purchase but then they do not take the excess capital and invest it. If you are in this situation you can always take a half position by financing ½ of the purchase and pay cash for the other half. That way you are not all in or all out.

In financing appreciating assets like a home you really end up getting some leverage if the home appreciates over time. People don't usually think of it in those terms but if you buy a home for $160,000 and put down 20% ($32,000), the balance that you owe is $128,000. If the home appreciates 3% per year for the next 10 years the home would be worth $216,026. Even though you haven't paid off the mortgage loan you are participating in the appreciation of the $128,000 that you owe on the home. If you want to sell the home you get the $216,026, less your real estate selling fees and the current value that you owe on your home. Part of your payments during those 10 years go to both interest and principle. The principle portion is what you get back at the time of sale which is included in the $216,026 above. That is the benefit of financing an appreciating asset!

55 *Buy Stocks wisely*

We have all gotten so excited to purchase something we just blurt out the words "I'll take it", without even giving much thought to the price that we will have to pay. Almost no one would buy a house or a car without asking the price and just saying, "I'll take it," only to find out what the purchase price was later. Most people want to know the exact price of a home or car prior to purchase and agree to pay a specific price or make an offer of what they are willing to pay. If the seller agrees to that price offer a sale is made.

It works the same way in the stock market. Two different types of orders to buy or sell stock are limit orders and market orders. A limit order is an order that gives a specific price that you are willing to buy or sell for a particular stock. If someone is willing to sell at a price that you offer to buy then a sale is made and you own the stock at that exact price. With a market order you are basically saying, "I'll take it", and this order turns into a sale at an unknown price until the sale is done. When putting in a market order to buy something someone willing to sell may raise their price unusually high because they see your order to buy at any price. Therefore use limit prices when buying or selling stock on most of your transactions. There are some exceptions in which you are trading a stock that has a huge market and high trading volumes. General Electric is one that trades frequently and a lot of volume so a market order may not matter as it would be too difficult to manipulate. If you absolutely have to get out of a stock position immediately you may have to put in a market order to liquidate the position, just know going into the trade that you will not get a favorable price.

When prices are quoted it is generally based on the price of the most recent trade; however, there is something called the bid/ask spread. These are the prices the professionals see. The bid price is the immediate buy price if someone places a market order to buy. The ask price is the immediate sell price if someone were to place a market order to sell. The difference between the bid price and ask price is generally a lot larger in stocks that trade a lower volume of shares. Stocks that trade a high volume of shares usually have a fairly close bid to ask spread.

Also understand what the Beta is of a stock that you are

buying. The Beta is the calculation or value of a stock in relation to the S&P500. The S&P500 has a Beta of exactly 1 as it is equal to itself. If a stock has a beta of .85 it would move up or down only 85% of the markets movement. If a stock had a beta of 2 it would generally move 2 times as much as the market or double the volatility.

SECTION 3: SAVING

Secret Principles

"I've got all the money I'll ever need if I die by 4 O'clock tomorrow" - Henny Youngman

56 *Discover your top 3 expenses throughout the year. Focus on cutting 2 of those expenses by 10% each.*

This can certainly be a challenge; however, if you do not try to cut the major expenses you may never get a good handle on managing these. You should be able to identify these top expenses fairly quickly, if not this exercise should certainly cause you to think about it. If you can save 10% on each of your top 2 expenses a year it should free up a fair amount of money every month for you to start investing. One example of this that I used years ago while living alone in my first home was to rent my spare bedroom. The rent allowed someone else to share in my monthly mortgage payment. For me it ended up being a 25% savings per month on my largest expense, my home mortgage. Now you may look into refinancing your mortgage and find that you cannot save any money. If that is the case start to look at your next 2 expenses and see what you can do on those expenses. If you do look at refinancing your mortgage remember to not only compare your current payment to a new refinanced payment, but look at the amount of principle that you will be paying every month on each payment. The principle amount is the amount that you should look at as paying to yourself. If you can lower your payment by refinancing, but you lower the principle part of the payment as well, it may not be a savings to you overall in the end.

57 *Create separate accounts for upcoming expenses.*

Creating separate accounts for future expenses will help you budget money both physically and mentally. The items that I am referring to are things like vacations, clothes, gifts, a car, or other major purchases. You can set up bank accounts or simply keep an envelope in a filing cabinet for shorter term events or items. Years ago I set up bank accounts for my daughters that were car funds for them. We started very small with only $50.00, but it was a start and the money would not be spent on anything other than their 1st car. This exercise can create discipline and alleviates you from feeling a big financial burden when you go on a trip or have a larger than normal expense.

58 *Make payments to yourself.*

When making a car payment or other payment on a significant item, you typically have a monthly payment. Most people of course get into the habit of paying their payment every month. If you are in that habit and can keep that habit of payments going once your loan is paid off, you will now be the one benefitting every month. Try to continue to make the same payment amount to yourself and put the money into an investment account for your next car or other major purchase. Once we get into the habit of doing something over time, it can be fairly easy to keep it going. Just think about the all the money you paid for your car over the past 2 or 3 years and think about all that money being in an account for you in the future.

59 *Negotiate on major purchases.*

Whenever you are making a major purchase like a house, car, or vacation, always negotiate. You will often be surprise how much you can save by taking your time and being patient. A couple percent savings can equate to thousands of dollars on expensive items. Many people think negotiating is wrong or rude or that you have to be a jerk in doing it. That is not true at all. I have found that you actually will do much better by being polite and asking nicely. I will use words like "can you please help me….?," "if you can do this for me I would greatly appreciate it, can you?" Asking a simple question like, "Is that the best price I can get?" will often get you several percent off a purchase.

Also be willing to take your time in the major purchases. It is perfectly acceptable to say you need to sleep on it and you will get back to them tomorrow. If someone pressures you to buy on that day, or saying the price is only good for that day, I have found that to be untrue and unnecessary sales pressure. They will be just as happy the next day to sell the product or service at that lower price.

Think about how much your time is worth as well. If you have to work several weeks for $2,000 and can save that amount of money by taking an extra half an hour on the purchase of a car you would be using your time very well. Too often I see people rush on major purchases and end up costing themselves hundreds and thousands of dollars unnecessarily.

60 *Create "DO NOT Touch" accounts.*

An IRA (Individual Retirement Account), is an account set-up specifically for retirement and has some legal features built in so you "Do Not" spend it until retirement. IRA's have penalty fees if you take money out of your account prior to 59 ½ years of age. You should try to set up an investment account or accounts that you plan to not touch or withdraw money out of until a specific time or for a specific purpose. Several types of accounts would be a first or new home account, a college saving account for children, or a new car account. When you set these up use your planning techniques to keep you discipline in not spending these unless an absolute dire emergency. These types of accounts allow you to mentally separate your money for different purposes and not have easy access to it and spend it on things that are not as important as the initial purpose of the money.

61 *Avoid hidden banking fees.*

Review your bank statements for hidden fees. Also talk with your bank about what you need to do to avoid these fees, have them removed, or even shop for a new bank. The charges can be a significant portion of the value of your account over time so a small investment of your time will be worth it to you. Sitting down face-to-face with someone at the bank can help you understand the charges clearly and they are generally more willing to help you if they have seen you before. The banking laws are changing and many banks will now start charging for checking accounts.

Banks made up to $8.7 billion a year in hidden fees called interchange bank fees, mostly on credit card processing to retailers. They may no longer be able to charge these fees in the future however.

You may want to look at credit unions that offer about every service as a bank at must lower fees to the members. They are very inexpensive to join and offer free checking. You can find a credit union close to your location at the National Credit Union Administration website, www.NCUA.gov .

62 *Learn to say "I can't afford it"*

Don't be embarrassed to say the words "I can't afford it," It is actually a good habit to get in to and admit that something is not within the current budget. I have gotten in the habit of saying that I can't afford things and I hear people say, "yeah right." Even though I have the money available it doesn't mean I can afford certain things because they are not in my plan or I didn't set money aside for that purchase. In keeping that discipline I have found that it makes it easier every time I make the statement that I can't afford something. I am not embarrassed about it but have become proud of the discipline.

Have you ever noticed that people that are generally frivolous with money are the ones that don't have wealth? People that are tight or discipline with money generally have wealth. I wonder why that is?

63 *Lower your insurance costs*

Lowering your insurance cost is a great way to save on money that you are already spending. There are several ways to lower your auto insurance costs. You can certainly shop other companies to see if they will lower your fees and change insurance companies. Avoiding traffic tickets and accidents is one of the best ways of course. You may just call your insurance company and make sure you are getting all the discounts that you are eligible for, such as safe driver discount or good student discounts. Another great way to save money is to raise your deductible. Raising your deductible from $200 to $500 can save hundreds per year and more than off-set the increased deductible in savings to you per year. You may consider dropping collision coverage on and older car as well as the insurance company's only give current replacement value on cars that are totaled in an accident.

If renting a car do not pay for the insurance that the car rental company offers as you are generally covered by your primary auto insurance company.

If you have homeowner's insurance combine your auto and home owners insurance with the same company as this can save up to 10% savings. As on your auto insurance you can increase that deductible on you homeowners insurance. Raising the deductible from $200 to $1000 can save 15% to 20% per year. Also make sure you are getting all the discounts for things like alarm systems, security doors, and fire alarms. You may even call the insurance company and see what items they consider in offering discounts as they may list some that you are not aware of. There is a reason insurance companies advertise so much on TV. They make a lot of money on consumers. Don't give them any more than you have to.

64 *Warning! Taxes may be hazardous to your wealth.*

Taxes can eat a huge chunk of our income over time. Therefore it is important to focus on keeping as much of our income and money we legally can. The best way to do this is to keep good records at the start of the year and throughout the year. Too many people wait until filing their taxes to start to think about savings. It is often much too difficult for people to hunt down receipts on expenses when the tax year has passed.

A simple task of keeping separate files or envelopes for expenses like health care, recording mileage for work or a job search, and donations is a way to start to take advantage of benefits that are due to you. Here are some categories for tax files or receipt envelopes:

- All auto expenses if used at all for business, including mileage, license & registration, and maintenance.
- Healthcare costs, insurance and any out of pocket medical.
- Entertainment related to business.

- Phone records if phone is used for business.
- Clothing costs for employment related uniforms.
- Travel costs relating to business, auto rentals, hotels, and meals.
- Office supplies, mailing, equipment, and software that are business related.
- Donations, both monetary and clothing or other items.

Other ways to cut your tax deductions or defer taxes are to take advantage of IRA's and setting up a 529 college saving plan that allows grow of the plan to grow tax free as long as the 529 funds are used for education.

Check the department of revenue's web site of the state that you reside in to see what tax credits are available for you as well. A tax credit is a dollar for dollar reduction of the tax you owe at the end of the year, while a deduction is a reduction prior to the tax being calculated. If you have considerable health care costs consider setting up a Health Savings Account (HSA). The IRS lets you contribute about $6,200 per year as pretax funds, and they allow you to use the funds in future years toward healthcare costs. You will need to do your own calculations and talk to a tax professional to see if it will work for you. Even if you file your own taxes it is a good idea to talk with a tax professional to get sound advice and have current year information.

*The above should not be considered personal tax advice or individual recommendations. Always talk with a qualified tax professional or consult the IRS directly prior to making personal tax decisions.

65 *Reduce gas and groceries costs*

There are several ways to save on both gas and groceries and also help combine the savings. Many grocery stores have clubs or valued shopper programs. Be sure to join these programs to get the discount on many of the items in the store that are offered. Try to buy those items that offer the special club price discount. Many of these grocery stores also now have discount gas programs with their own gas stations or some are partnered with the major oil companies. Be sure to ask as you can save close to a dollar per gallon if you buy enough groceries and catch the double rewards offered several times per year.

There are also smart phone apps that will help you shop for the cheapest gas as well that include maps of stations near you. This can help you save 5 or 10 cents per gallon. Just don't drive 12 miles out of your way to get cheaper gas. You should also check with the manufacturer of your automobile to see what type of gas they recommend. They may recommend a premium grade. If they do you should follow their recommendation, as even though it is more expensive you will get better mileage with higher grade fuels. Also it is a good idea to put in fuel additive or fuel cleaners a couple times per year as they will help clean fuel injectors and help you get better gas mileage. These can be found at most auto stores or in auto departments at many major retailers. Check your tire pressure as well and keep it at the recommend psi level on the side of the tire. A tire with low air pressure requires more fuel to travel.

Practicing good driving habits can help save about 5 to 10% on fuel consumption. Try to combine trips, for example if dropping your children off to school or friends stop at the store on the way back or when coming home from work make required stops then. Also driving smooth and use your cruise control can save 10% on your gas usage. Fast acceleration is one of the biggest gas hogs you can do. Try to use carpooling as a way to save on gas when you can. Take a bike for short trips when you are alone if you can, not only will it save gas but you get exercise as well.

Lastly, you can even keep a log to see how many miles to a tank of gas you can get at least a few times. Try to set a new record with every tank.

66 *Reduce utility bills*

Our monthly power bill is generally a sizeable portion of our monthly expenses, so chipping away at reducing this recurring cost can really pay over time. The first thing you should do is to call your power company or go to their website to explore the various ways to save on your electric bill. One way may be to simply change your billing that allows for half priced or reduced fee power between 9pm and 9am. If you choose this type of plan you will want to run major power consuming devices during the lower rate times. Major power device are things like clothes dryer, pool filters, air conditioning and heating units. If you make a conscious effort it can really help reduce your monthly bill. A load controller is a device that connects into your circuit breaker and shuts off appliances if there is too big a draw or power spike. Investing in a load balancer can also pay for itself over time and some power companies have given credit on utility bills for the purchase of a load controller. Also most power companies offer good suggestions on their web sites regarding sealing your home well in your windows, doors and other openings. Balancing your home in terms of keeping each room the same temperature is becoming more popular recently as well.

Other things that can be done to insure the lowest possible utility bill every month are to, replace air filters regularly, get a new smart thermostat, (these now have self-learning built into them to regulate the temperature of you home while you are home and away), make sure you have plenty of insulation in your attic, and use single room space heaters if you spend most of your time in a particular room in your home.

There are other cleaver devices out there that can help reduce your bill. One of which is a dryer add-on device that put the hot dryer air after filtering, back into your home instead of heating it and blowing it out of your home.

Things you can do are to turn off lights when leaving a room for over 10 minutes. Also install newer energy efficient light bulbs and wear a sweater when cold instead of turning up the heat. Many people are unaware that appliances can still use up to 70% of the power consumption when still plugged in but in the "off" mode. So if you can unplug things when not in use for extended periods you will help save on power consumption that way as well. Or you can make it a bit easier by plugging them into a power strip and turning off the power strip when not in use.

67 *Reduce phone bills*

Home phone costs have generally gone down over the past 15 years; however, the cost of cell phones has taken away more than the savings. If you are still paying long distance fees on your home phone you can certainly reduce these fees by using various internet services provided that you are already paying for internet at home. One of the ways is to use, *Skype*, for long distance calls over the internet. They have several free services and also some fee based services that are very reasonable if you make a lot of calls or use a lot of minutes. *Ooma* is another solution that uses the internet and will allow you to cancel your home phone line and the line cost altogether. It actually allows you to use your current home phone as well and even keep your same number. The way it works is this; it is a small box that plugs into your home internet modem and also plugs into your home phone line. The box has an initial cost; however, you no longer have the monthly fee from the phone company nor any long distance charges.

If you have a current mobile phone service like most of use you can do several things to reduce your fee. The first and easiest is to call your provider or go into one of their stores and ask them if they can reduce your plan. With the fierce competition between providers and new lower rates and packages constantly coming out to the market they are forced to try to keep up with each other and we the consumer benefit. Recently I walked into the local store and by asking this simple question I saved over $20 per month on my bill, but they didn't seek me out and voluntarily tell me I could pay less. Also try to get on plan together with family members sharing the plans as that can also bring a significant savings in your bill. Some companies will allow you to share data plans or texting plans saving over 20% from having them individually. Also ask your provider to help optimize your plan so you are not paying the expensive overage charges for data or texting. They should be able to put you on a plan that is optimal for your average monthly usage.

68 *Repair first before replacing*

My car recently had a bad battery; my 15 year old daughter's solution was to go get a new vehicle. That is certainly a dramatic solution to a minor problem and certainly more expensive. If something you own breaks, consider fixing it or having it repaired prior to buying a new item. Cars are certainly an easy example that we can look at that need ongoing servicing and repairs. Most of us have many things that can be fixed to extend the useful life of the product. A vacuum cleaner is a great example of something that people buy new when a three dollar belt and cleaning may get it running close to new. It is often a wise idea to have something repaired prior to selling it, as it will be much easier to sell when it is in good working condition. Generally it is pretty easy to get an estimate on repairs on things like refrigerators, washing machines, dryers, computers etc. One of the most common reasons people buy new computers is that their current computer is slow. That information comes from BestBuy who loves to sell people new computers. People often don't take the simple steps to get their computer running faster by doing some inexpensive things like upgrading the memory, cleaning the disk, and reloading various programs. So before you just go buy a new computer take some easy steps to get your computer running in top shape. The easy fixes are to upgrade the memory, scan for viruses, defragment your disk drive, and delete old unused programs. A bigger step is to clean the disk and then restore your data files, including your programs. This takes much more time and does require and expert on computers.

YouTube has great information on fixing and repairing things for free. It is surprising some of the solutions that people have come up with and their willingness to share such useful information at no cost. Take the time to look up something that you need, just fixed, or replaced to see the vast information available to you.

69 *Live within your means*

This simple statement is something that many people fail to do even the people running our government. What does this mean? The statement means that you should not spend more money than you make. Many people cannot seem to exercise the daily discipline necessary to spend less than they make and live below their current income or means. There are only 2 outcomes if someone continues to outspend their income: 1) They realize that they don't have the money to pay the bills and they take action to correct the issue by making more or spending less or 2) They continue to live 'above' their means, spending more than they make and end up bankrupt, unable to pay their bills, and in debt. I call this running the car into the wall without taking your foot off the gas pedal.

It is statistically accurate that the more than half the people that win the lottery are broke within 5 years. Why? Most likely they psychologically think that the money can never run out and they do not take into consideration taxes or track their spending. Many wealthy actors and athletes have ended up bankrupt spending or wasting tremendous wealth without discipline. So just having a lot of money is not the entire answer.

Walt Disney, Mark Twain, & Mike Tyson all have something in common; they all filed bankruptcy at one point in their lives. Mike Tyson did after making more than $300 million. He is now an advocate trying to help others learn from his lesson.

70 *Sell non-used items*

My daughters and I have sold many old items that they have out grown on craigslist raising money for other things they needed or wanted. It just takes a little creativity and digging around the house to find things that you don't use or value personally any longer. Although you may not value them they may have value to someone else. If you question whether or not someone would buy your item or you are unsure of the value, just go onto Craigslist or EBay and see what similar items are selling for. We have sold things from stuffed animals, a back yard play-set, desks, a trampoline, old cell phones, a prom dress, computer, refrigerator, a car, jet-ski lifts, and more.

It has surprised me how easy it has been to sell some of the items that I would have just thrown away or given away. It has also motivated my daughters to put some effort into getting something ready to sell so they can make some money toward the purchase of something they have been saving for or wanting.

If you haven't done this before you can meet people at a local coffee shop to sell smaller items or even meet them at a neutral location prior to having them come to your home so you feel safer. I have actually met very nice people along the way.

It is fairly easy to place the ads on Craigslist or EBay. You should remind the buyers that the buyers don't have to pay sales tax when buying from a private party. Look at some other people's ads that you like and you can write yours just like the ones that you like and include the information that is needed to interest buyers. Photos are necessary and easy now with most cell phones having built in cameras. Most people pay in cash and I would not take a check unless you met them at the bank. If it an expensive item like a car you will want to go to a bank to verify funds and possibly get the title notarized there as well.

Educate yourself and give it a try, my guess is that you will be surprised at what you can sell and the amount of money you can raise with a little effort.

71 Pay down debt

You should develop the mind-set of paying down any debt you have prior to spending money on any non-emergency expenses. You should also pay down your highest interest rate debts first as they simply cost you more money in terms of interest every month. You should look at the interest expense as money you can put into your pocket or spend on something else you need. Once you get your debt paid off you'll be in a situation to have more money to spend or invest. The mistake many people make is carrying credit card debt at over 10% interest while continuing to spend more money on things they do not really need. Try to get into the habit of using the credit card only if you can pay it off at the end of the month.

Pay down debt on anything except your home as your home has a mortgage amortization that has the interest portion of the loan pay-down built in to the loan. Most car loans are structured the same way with less interest being paid every month until the loan matures.

If you have significant debt that you are having difficulty in paying off you can contact a debt consolidator and they can roll various debts and loans into a simple loan with 1 payment per month. Debt consolidators should be used as a last resort as they are expensive and can carry a lot of hidden fees. Depending on your credit rating they can often offer much better interest rates than credit card companies and can extend the term lowering the amount you have to pay every month. This may be a good way to go if you can stay discipline and not dig yourself deeper into debt.

72 *Seek Support*

Tell your family and people close to you that you are trying to save money and cut unnecessary expenses. Ask them to hold you accountable and let you know if they see you doing any unnecessary spending. It may annoy you at times but there is nothing like getting the truth to help you reach your goals.

Most successful people will tell you that they have trusted advisors close to them that tell them things they do not want to hear on occasion but expect to hear the truth. A different perspective helps them avoid big mistakes and keeps them moving toward the goal.

It has been said that smart Generals never go to war without seeking advice on all aspects prior to engaging. Even Saddam Hussain had a General, George Sadda, who would tell Hussain when he thought the plans would fail. Hussain didn't like him but respected him for standing up and telling the truth.

Sometimes it takes another person's view to take a different perspective on what we are doing and give us some honest advice. Often we can be too close to the situation to make good sound, solid decisions.

73 *Use your free resources*

You have a tremendous resource at your disposal that is free for you to use all day long 6 days a week. Your local library is a tremendous free benefit to you and allows you to borrow books instead of buying them. Not only does this save a lot of money for you but you can gain knowledge from experts in areas that you want to learn more about. If you want to start a business, for example, you can find some books on that topic. When people are in the library they are more likely to check out a book that looks somewhat interesting than buy a book and commit to it if it is not exactly what they want.

Many people these days are seeking a quiet place to get away for a while. It doesn't have to be an expensive vacation or a beach location. You can just go to the library for a few hours to get some solitude and recharge yourself in a good book.

If reading is not really 'your thing,' most libraries now even have books on MP3 that you can download to your favorite player so you can just sit back and listen to helpful or interesting books. This can be a great way to pass time while driving. You can also get a variety of movies at most libraries for free as well. They generally have a good selection of documentaries and a reasonable selection of more popular family movies. If you are someone that tends to rent a lot of movies this can save you hundreds of dollars per year. "Check-it-out" for yourself!

74 *Protect your private information and assets*

One area that can be overlooked in saving money is protecting you from unseen costs. One that is more prevalent now than ever is identity thief. Most of us have heard of someone or may even know someone that has had their identity stolen in some way. Having anything stolen like an account or credit card can be costly in terms of money and time. It can take months to try and eliminate issues in the event of stolen assets.

Some of the best ways to protect yourself these days are by protecting access to important documents and information. At a minimum you should have a locking mail box at your home. If you don't lock your mailbox someone can easily steal your mail which may include bank statements or brokerage statements. You should have a document shredder at your home to shred any important documents that have any confidential information like your social security number or driver license number that someone could misuse. Also subscribing to an identity prevention service like LifeLock is a good idea and added protection for you as well.

You may want to consider adding an umbrella insurance policy to your homeowner's insurance policy. This type of coverage is fairly low cost for the added insurance it gives you in almost any situation above and beyond general homeowners or car insurance.

Simple things like making sure your home and car are locked when they should be can prevent easy access. Upgrading your home with security doors and an alarm system may lower the probability of being vandalized. When parking your car for any length of time do not leave any valuables visible in the vehicle. Many people have had windows broken and a purse taken right off the car seat when just gone for 10 minutes. Do not underestimate the bad guys. A few minutes of prevention can save you hours of trying to fix the problem by some wrong doer.

75 *Shop at a dollar store*

Try shopping at a dollar store to see if there are items in there that you have bought and paid much more for someplace else. You may be surprised to find brand name items there selling for one dollar. I'm not saying all items in there are high quality but I admit seeing brand name, quality items in certain areas.

I found some consumable items in which quality did not matter as much were acceptable to me. I found that I didn't care to spend significantly more for things like disposable plastic food containers, paper bags, dental floss, detergent, glass cleaner, and drain cleaner. I'm just using these products for a very short product life time so paying 3 or 4 times as much as these items at another store did not show value to me.

You may want to stay away from certain items and categories like food, medicine, and vitamins to be on the safe side as the risk/reward may not be worth it. However, you will probably find some items that you are already buying and paying much more for allowing you to save some money pretty easily.

76 *You are not saving money by spending money*

When looking at something, "on sale," don't fall into the trap of thinking, "how much will I save?," think about how much money you are about to spend and what it will be worth in 5 years if invested properly. Department stores have done studies and found that by marking the prices up on items then marking them down as if, "on-sale," they sell faster. They create a false perception of saving money.

Now if you were going to buy an item anyhow and you get it at a discount that is better than paying full price; however, the point I'm trying to get across is that you should not buy something thinking you are saving money. The only way to truly save is by not spending the money and investing it. If you didn't need an item at full price you probably don't need it just because it is less expensive now and you may end up regretting the purchase down the road. Beware of trying to, "save," money by spending.

77 *Avoid payment penalties*

Most penalty fees can be avoided with a bit of thoughtful planning. There are emergencies that are clearly the exception; however, most expenses can be reduced or avoided with some thinking and action ahead of time.

Penalties are common in bank accounts that are over drawn, on credit cards, and bills that are paid late. The penalty fees can be expensive based on the percentage of funds in a bank account or on the total due on a bill. By making sure you don't over draw on your bank accounts and by paying your bills on time you can avoid these expensive and unnecessary fees.

Do everything you can to not withdraw money early from a retirement account because they have a penalty fee. Most retirement accounts, IRA's and 401K's, have a 10% penalty for taking money out prior to the qualified retirement age.

You are generally better off taking out a low interest loan than paying a 10% penalty on your retirement account as you hurt your future by paying extra now to have funds that would grow into retirement. That 10% penalty will not be easy to make up over time in term of dollar value.

There are some exceptions in which you can withdraw funds early which include disability, medical over 10% of your adjusted gross income, qualified first-time home buyers, higher education costs (for yourself and even family members), health insurance costs if unemployed, and a few others that you should check with the IRS or your tax expert in the appropriate tax year if you are considering an early withdrawal. Be sure to check with your tax preparer as tax laws change year to year and everyone's situation is different.

SECTION 4: SPENDING

Secret Principles

Proverbs 13:7 - One man pretends to be rich, yet has nothing; another pretends to be poor, yet has great wealth.

78 *Write down 3 things you have bought in the past couple years that you wish you didn't buy and would rather have the money now.*

We can all look back at something we bought in a weak moment or out of compulsive behavior with regret. If you had taken more time to think about your purchases you may not have bought some of them and you would now have the money saved, invested, and growing for your future. This should help you make better purchases toward your needs in the future. Better yet, the investment may be working out quite well. This exercise will hopefully get you to think a bit more prior to making a hasty purchase. I used this exercise on my daughter, (14 years old at the time), asking her if she would like to have that 100 dollars now that she had spent on various toys. She said, "Of course, Dad, I wish I saved some of that money and had it now," I replied, "You will probably feel the same way in a few years so think carefully about how you spend your money now." I can see that she is now putting in more thinking prior to purchases based on this lesson.

79 *Try to limit your debt to your home. Home mortgages are generally the lowest interest rates available and part of your payment is tax deductible.*

Credit card debt is generally the worst debt you can have due to the high interest rates. So you want to get credit cards paid off as soon as you possibly can and avoid occuring credit card debt whenever possible. Some credit cards charge over 15% annually on the money that you don't pay off every month. Try to look at any debt as paying yourself the interest on the debt if you can pay it off. A general rule of thumb is to pay cash for depreciating assets and finance appreciating assets. It is not always easy to know which ones appreciate over time, but housing is one that historically does well over the long-term of 10 years or more. Cars, furniture, home appliances, and clothes are some of they types of assets that depreciate over time. It is ok to have debt on your home in the form of your mortgage as home loan rates are generally the lowest form of interest rate that consumers can get and a portion of the home loan is tax deductible to most people. (Note: please check with your tax preparer or accountant regarding your personal tax situation)

80 *Proceed with caution prior to large purchases.*

Before making a purchase of $100 or more, write down 3 reasons why you need it or want it and then wait at least 7 days prior to purchasing it. If it is still important after 7 days you may really need it. This exercise has stopped me from spending money too freely and can slow down your spending as well. One of the key elements in this exercise is to *stop the emotional purchases* that we make without giving much thought to them. I was surprised to learn that many times after only waiting 3 days to purchase an item that I really wanted earlier, I had already lost quite a bit of interest in it. If you do feel that you really need something or that it is an emergency and cannot wait, be sure to keep the receipt so you can take it back if you realize later that it really wasn't a need but only a want. My teen daughters easy confuse "need" and "emergency" far too often. Define an emergency long before you think you have one.

81 *Learn to use sites on the internet to find the lowest price on items.*

Shopping on the internet can certainly have advantages and save you money. Using sites like Amazon or Groupon can save significant money in percentage terms. I have often found used items on Amazon that appear new to me but sell for half-price as used; many books fall into that category. Craigs-list also has a tremendous amount of products that people often just hope to get rid of and can save a fraction of the price of a new item. Remember that you may have to pay shipping when purchasing from some sites. Therefore, factor shipping into the total price prior to purchasing an item. Some higher priced items often include free shipping to help make the overall purchase price more competitive with local stores. Some stores will even allow you to order via the internet and pick it up at the store. That way you do not pay for the shipping on the item and you get the "Internet price," which is almost always less than or equal to the "store price."

Be sure to use the internet for your travel related expenses. There are some great sites out there that will shop for the best price on airline tickets or hotel rooms. Check various websites before booking your travel. Checks airline web sites and discount web sites prior to purchasing as the airline web site is occasionally the same or lower than discount sites. Priceline.com is the big one, but there are others like Kayak, Experian, and Hotels.com to compare too also. If you are staying in a location for more than a couple days you may check VRBO.com., (Vacation Rental By Owner) for homes and condos for rent. I have found great places with full kitchens and multiple bedrooms for less than a hotel room.

82 *Keep your receipts and purchase records.*

We have all heard someone in our lives say, "I just don't know where all my money goes." You may be in this group or have at least 1 foot in it like most of us. We can all get a little better understanding of our purchasing habits by reviewing our purchases each month.

Keep your receipts of all purchases in various categorized envelopes. For example keep and envelope marked dining out, one for clothes, and one for gas. At the end of each year add these up to see how much you are spending in various categories. You can even do this at the end of each month to get a better handle and understanding of where you are spending your money. Hind sight, as they say is 20/20, therefore when looking back on how you spend your money, you will be better prepared to make good decisions going forward. Don't be afraid to take something back that you realized you did not need or that you may have purchased by mistake. If you have the receipt it will make it a lot easier for you. You should not be embarrassed returning an item that does not fit or work for you for any other reason. Returning an item is not personal and the clerk in the store will not care either way. Businesses want you to be a satisfied customer.

83 *Think in terms of percentage saving.*

When buying any item start looking at the purchase in terms of percentages of your earnings or savings. Viewing things differently can open our eyes to new ways of doing things. This method of thinking is exactly how the top financial minds at top companies think. Many people make impulse decisions on small purchases. They then get into the habit of thinking that if an item is under $10 it's not worth the time to try to and get it for a lower price. Many items in that price range may differ by 20% or more which is a very large percentage difference. Now you may be saying, "yes, but $8 or $10 is not a big deal." However, if you make this type of decision only 4 times per week on 4 items it will certainly add up. Let's do the math: $2 X 4 times per week = $8 per week, $8 X 52 weeks in a year = $416, doing this over 10 years = **$4,160!** That number does not include any interest or return had you invested it wisely either. Just an interest rate of 5% over that time would put your saving at **$5,232!** So does it pay over time to shop a bit for a lower price? I certainly think so. The above example is only based on 1 item as well, just think about an entire grocery cart of products and the savings over time. I understand convenience and the habit we can easily get into to save a little time; however, too often people pay 15% to 20% more for a small time savings that just gets used up by sitting on the couch watching TV. That is not time or money well spent.

84 *Buy your next car used from a private party.*

People often ask whether they should buy or lease a vehicle. There is not an easy answer that fits everyone. If you have to have a new car then your options are to buy or lease. The broad based rule is to lease if you know that you will not want the vehicle for more than the term of the lease and that you will not drive over the mileage allowance. If you plan to keep a vehicle for a period longer than the term of the lease you will be better off buying the vehicle. You should also finance as little as possible when buying a car in most situations. Financing factors will depend on your ability to put some money down and also the interest rate being charged.

The auto industry is very aware that the majority of a new automobile's depreciation is in the first 2 years. That is why leases are structured the way they are on new cars. The payments over the term of the lease cover all the depreciation of the vehicle over the lease period. The dealers know this and if they have to take the vehicle back after the lease they know they have already captured the depreciation value via the lease payments.

Buying a used car will allow you to get a car that has had a large portion of depreciation on someone else's wallet instead of yours. When buying from a private party you will save on taxes because you don't have to pay sales tax to a private party. Car dealers have to charge you tax on the sale of a used car as well as a new car in most states.

Most people do not think about the taxes on a vehicle prior to the purchase. This can be true even if you finance the car, as the taxes are generally added into the monthly payments. Taxes can be around 9% in some states. If you buy a vehicle from a dealer that costs $20,000 the tax at 9% on the vehicle is an additional $1,800. That is a significant amount added to the overall cost. Think about applying that $1,800 tax saving to the cost of a vehicle from a private party. You may get a better quality vehicle without spending more than you would at a dealership. There are many ways to find private party auto sales; Cars.com, AutoTrader.com, and Craigslist. You may even find them in parking lots with for sale signs on them.

85 *Be consistent by making good purchasing decisions.*

"It isn't hard to be good from time to time. What's tough is being good every day." - Willie Mays

Pay attention to the small purchases and strive to make wise decisions on them so you will be in the good-habit when making larger purchases. There is an interesting story about billionaire Warren Buffett golfing with some friends. They all came to a short hole and someone suggested betting $10 each if someone got a hole-in-one on that hole. All the players said yes to the bet except Warren Buffett. Someone later said to Mr. Buffett, "Warren why did you pass on that bet? It was only $10, that's nothing to you." Mr. Buffett replied something like this. "The odds of getting a hole-in-one are so terrible that it would not be a good use of the $10, and if I allow myself to make poor decisions on a small amount of money I may end up making a poor decision on a large amount of money at some point." You see Mr. Buffett did not let greed take over or emotions get involved in his decision, he stopped and thought about the probability and whether it was a good use of his $10. Good decisions with money have become engraved in his character, his attitude, and his actions. Start making good decisions and choices on small matters with your money every day. The discipline will have a positive affect on your larger decisions as well.

86 *"Beware of little expenses. A small leak will sink a great ship."*
- Ben Franklin

I have certainly heard more than one person say, "I just don't know where all the money went." Look at some real-life examples of people that had millions and thought the money would never run out yet they end up having to file bankruptcy. Famed football player Tony Dorsett was in this boat and so was heavy weight champion Mike Tyson. It is often easy to lose track of your money and have nothing to show for it when they are just small expenses because psychologically we don't add them up as we go along spending. The first step is finding and identifying the leak.

As Ben Franklin points out above even big ships need to be concerned about small leaks. That is why you need to be concerned with small recurring expenses as they can sink your financial success. Try to keep a running list of the small expenses and put a weekly or monthly limit on what you will allow on the, "small expenses." You may be surprised at how easily they add up and can get away from you. Now having said that also be careful that you don't pick up nickels in front of freight trains so to speak. Meaning you can be so focused on saving a few pennies that you are spending dollars trying to save them. Be smart about saving and not costing yourself more in the long run. We have all probably experienced this in buying an inexpensive similar brand product only to find that we had to buy 2 times as much or that the product only lasted half the time. Try to find the smart balance and stop the leaks.

87 *Keep a written log of all that you spend for 1 month*

Keep a written log of all of your spending for a month. I realize this may be a bit of a pain at first. I suggest getting a small booklet to log in and keep it with you as the results will be a big eye opener. Another way to do it is to keep every receipt and write them down on a note pad at the end of every day. Over the period of a month you will get a good feel for where your money is going and what you are spending it on. You can also categorize your spending into *fixed expenses* and *variable expenses* every month once you have the log of expenses in front of you. You may want to categorize your list by entertainment, clothing, food, and one in which you track debt while spending. After the habit of doing this exercise for a month, you should start to visualize your overall spending a lot better, and also understand your spending by individual categories. In future months try to trim the list of expenses by 5 to 10%. Remember from previous sections that those savings invested properly over-time will grow far beyond just the amount saved.

88 *Stick to your list when shopping*

If you have a bad habit of buying things on impulse and often have buyer's remorse this exercise is for you. Before going shopping make of list of the items you, "need," not want, and only buy those items on your list. Don't buy on impulse or at least limit yourself to 2 items that are not on the list and define the maximum value prior to walking into the store. This principle could be paired with #9 that states small leaks can sink big ships. It is often too easy to put a few or more than a few extra items in the cart when shopping and not think ahead about the cost because they are just a few dollars each. It is often the impulse purchases that we end up paying a large premium for and we may not take the time to try and get a better price or value. The merchandise managers at the big stores know this and study people's habits and put items in high traffic areas knowing people will often make that thoughtless expensive decision. By having a list and sticking to it you will not fall prey to the over-priced purchases that you may have in the past. Implementing this principle may save you hundreds, or even thousands of dollars per year in some cases.

Just because you have money in your pocket doesn't mean you have to spend it.

Most of us can remember having some money in our pocket and being in a store looking for something to spend it on. The candy isle was and easy place for me. Even as people get older; however, they still find themselves in the habit of spending money just because they have it but then later regret it.

Spending money just because you have it is like looking for something to pound just because you have a hammer in your hand. Just be careful to think ahead so you don't have buyer's remorse and that you actually spend your money on something you really want and care about. We have already talked about good habits and it will get easier for you if you fight the urge to spend just because you have money in your pocket.

89 *Use coupons and rebates*

Coupons can often help you save an easy 10 to 50% by doing very little work. Some people check the paper every week and keep a small file box with them using only the coupons for things they intended to purchase anyhow. That is certainly worth the effort. You can also check online for coupons before purchasing larger value items. You'll be amazed at what you can find. There are now many companies that will accept electronic coupons off smart phones as well. Qponomics is a company offering mobile coupon service to consumers for locations from various services like car washes to restaurants.

When making a purchase that offers a rebate be sure to send the receipt and information required to get your rebate. I know when I purchase something that offers a rebate I buy based on the price after the rebate like most people. It has been stated by retailers that up to 30% of people that purchase items with rebates *do not even send in the required information* to get the offered rebate. That is pure laziness by consumers! A small task that takes only a few minutes to get a check for any amount is well worth the effort. After all if you really purchased the item with the price after rebate, you owe it to yourself to get the money back that the company offered to you.

90 *Time is Money*

"Waste neither time nor money, but make the best use of both." -Benjamin Franklin

Wealthy people look at how they spend their time validating the adage, ***that time is money***. The wealthy realize that time is valuable and that you cannot afford to waste it. Time should be viewed as the precious resource it is; as we cannot remake or recreate time. Once time is spent it is gone. You should be cognizant as to where and how you utilize your time and how much time you have to put into earnings. Look at the table below and see what the value of time is worth per minute based on annual income levels.

Annual Income	Time Value Per Minute
$5,000	$.06
$10,000	.11
$20,000	.22
$30,000	.34
$50,000	.56
$80,000	.90
$100,000	1.12
$200,000	2.24

When we look at this table it should help you realize just how valuable your time is and show that you really can't afford to waste much income producing time. Also it shows us again that pennies do make a difference as we saw in earlier compound interest examples. A few pennies more a minute can add up to a rather large difference in annual income and certainly over a lifetime.

91 *Money is stored work, effort, and labor*

Historically money has existed for a long time in some form. Prior to people exchanging paper money for goods and services they would trade, or barter, for their goods and services. If you needed someone to make your clothes you may have to offer many days of your labor in exchange for your clothes. This could be considered a form of an IOU if you received your clothes before your labor was completed. Money is a form of stored wealth or stored work and labor. In our society paper money makes it easy to transfer our work, effort, and labor to someone else for goods and services.

In understanding this fundamental principle, "that time is money," you may have a different outlook when spending your money. If you buy something on a credit card or go in debt you are really offering your future labor to get a product or service now. You will also pay a significant penalty if you don't pay off the credit card right away. So when you go to spend money on something ask yourself , "How long would it take me to work for this and pay for it?" Using the previous chart calculate the number of hours or days that you will work to pay for some of the things you buy. This exercise will help you understand the true value your precious time and efforts.

92 *Dining out smart*

Dining out can be very expensive and often not the time saver that many initially expect. Several expenses that many don't take into consideration when planning to dine out are drinks, taxes, and tips. These additional expenses can add up to 30% of the food bill and end up being a big surprise to many at the end of the meal when the check comes. Here are a few things you can do to make dining out more affordable. First make a list of restaurants with specials for every day of the week. When you do eat out you can go to the places that have "happy-hour prices," or offer a "2 for 1" special. You may want to share larger portions with your dining party cutting your cost and not wasting food. Also check restaurant web sites for coupons they offer and check Groupon.com for offers and discounts. Ordering a glass of water is also free and much healthier than most other drinks offered at restaurants.

The next time you cook meals at home write down how much you spend on the meal and how many people it feed. Using this idea compare it to the cost of eating that same meal out at a restaurant verse eating in for the same number of people. You can often eat in for less than half of what it would cost to eat out at a restaurant. I know that restaurant food taste good, but it is often at the cost of a lot of unhealthy butter or other products added as well. So you should be able to eat at home for less and generally eat much healthier.

93 *Find inexpensive hobbies and entertainment*

Some hobbies and activities can be very expensive, therefore understand how much you are spending per month on your hobbies and entertainment. Consider all factors of money you spend on hobbies such as equipment, travel to get there, replacement parts, food, and extra clothing. I have been fortunate to go on a number of scuba diving trips and I can assure you that it is not an inexpensive hobby when all expenses of travel and equipment are taken into consideration. Try to discover 2 new low cost hobbies that you enjoy like hiking or painting for example.

Entertainment can be very expensive for a family of 4. Just going to dinner and the movies can add up quickly on the average family, especially when you throw in some theater priced candy and popcorn. Instead you may try to eat at home and go to the movies bringing in your own candy from the store at the fraction of the cost. Another option is to go to dinner and then rent a movie and make your popcorn at home having a fun family evening. You can still do dinner and a movie but save some money in the process.

Reading is certainly one of the lowest costs of entertainment. Think of all the adventures you could have just reading a great book or places you can discover and topics you can learn about in detail while reading a good book. Of course books can provide great education and information on topics of interest as well.

94 *Think "used" first in purchases*

Always think "used" first in your purchases. This doesn't mean that buying something used will always be a better solution; however, this simple technique can save you thousands of dollars per year. You will be able to learn and take advantage of other peoples mistakes when they have purchased something that they can't afford and they need to liquidate it. People sell things that are virtually new in the box at half price because they just need to get rid of it. People move, get divorced, and have other life changes that cause them to sell possessions quickly. You do need to be careful in buying computers or things that may be dated a bit. Be sure to do some research on the item prior to your purchasing it. You can even search liquidation web sites for everything from new furniture to electronics. Many of these places make bulk purchases from companies that have gone out of business so they often have goods in a warehouse with low overhead that they can sell at deep discounts.

Something else that is becoming more popular is consignment stores for home goods and clothing. You may look for clothing exchange stores that will buy or sell your clothes on consignment. You may get store credit there as well for old clothes that you no longer want or wear. Using this principle can really save money unlike falling prey to the typical retailer that marks up prices only so they can put them "On-sale," creating an illusion of saving money for the consumer. You can feel good about repurposing items that other do not want.

95 *Build instead of buy*

Some things can be built by you for much less than buying a finished product at a store. I am fortunate to have a Mother that makes beautiful quilts. Not only are they much nicer than a blanket I could buy at a store, they are higher quality and more meaningful to me as well. Recently my daughter wanted a headboard for her bed. After we looked at the expensive headboards in stores she did not find the exact fabric she wanted and she suggested making one. I applauded her thinking, and then shortly after that I made some plans, bought some wood, and started to make the headboard. She shopped for fabric and other materials. The materials alone were much less expensive than one that we could have bought, and my daughter got the fabric she wanted and has something that is far more special to her than a store bought product. This is called "sweat equity!" I am certainly not all that handy but have made some things and they are always less expensive than the store bought version and have more personal value.

Another thing I have seen people do instead of buying expensive gifts is to make gifts for people. I have received various gifts that were hand-made and have much more meaning to me and my guess is that they cost less than a similar product in a store. So you may want to consider making something special and more meaningful as a gift for someone which often cost much less. If you have to give a lot of gifts it can be very cost effective to buy things in bulk from a craft store and put together several at once which brings the cost down significantly. My daughter just did this when making valentine ribbons for the troops. She did a great job on them and was able to make them for a lot of people very inexpensively with some personal sweat equity.

96 *Prepare for sales tax.*

Before spending money understand the extra money you will have to spend on sales tax as most states charge sales tax on everything you purchase. It can be a shock to people when they buy expensive items like automobiles or home furniture. Understand the total amount of money you will have to spend on those items not just what the price tag says. If you can understand those figures it will help you prepare mentally prior to making a purchase. Understand the total amount of money you have to earn before you pay income tax and prior to going to buy items. Spending less on items helps you lower the overall amount that you will pay in sales tax allowing you to keep more of your hard earned money.

For example let's say you can cut out $12,000 of spending per year. If your state sales tax is 8.5% you would save $1,020 just on sales tax that year. That is just one more good reason to curb your spending when you can.

97 *Understand that the small purchases add up over time.*

It is very easy for most of us to give very little thought to the small purchases day to day. But these small costs can really add up over time and cost you in the lack of invested assets as well. Just take the following example of buying a cup a coffee a day for $2.50 per day. That is probably a very low figure for many people. That totals $650 over the entire year. Think about the $650 being invested every year at just 5% annual interest. That $650 saved every year with a 5% return would be worth $4,421 after 5 years. After 10 years it would be worth $9,234. How much do you really like that coffee? Could you make your own coffee at home for much less?

Not everyone likes coffee but we all have little conveniences that we enjoy and they don't seem to cost very much day to day, but they can add up so we should pay attention to where are money is going over the long-term. The small expenses can be large costs over time or really add up into a nice sum if saved and invested wisely. Exercise: Try to find 1 or 2 ongoing expenses that you can at least trim by half, then save the money you would have spent.

98 *Systematic Spending*

Write out a monthly spending plan and stay within the limits. This exercise will help you understand where your money is being spent. You should see some fixed expenses like monthly mortgage or rent, car payments, and phone bills.

You will then have variable expenses like your power bill, clothes, entertainment, and dining out. In creating a written system, it should also help you set limits on things that vary each month like clothes, entertainment, and dining out. Put limits in place on these variable expenses which will be easier after you track them for several months. Let everyone in the family know the plan or they may overspend in certain categories. Also you can give everyone in the family their own limits and plan. This is a great way to build responsibility with children as well. They feel empowered and have some freedom with boundaries.

Track every expense to clearly understand where you are spending money. It is not difficult but will require a bit of discipline. You can get a small notebook to keep track of every expense every day or log it into an app on your smart phone. Get into the habit of asking for receipts when you make a purchase and keep them together so you can add them up later. Make sure you catch all expenses like ones that are automatically billed to a credit card every month or an automatic withdrawal from your checking account.

When getting your results after a couple months the first question you should ask yourself is, "Am I making more money than I am spending per month?" If the answer is no, something has to change and you are now better equipped to evaluate the area of expenses that need to be trimmed or cut.

I realize that this is not the glamorous part of becoming wealthy but it is a key and important step.

99 *Cash in while paying with cash.*

It can be much easier for most of us psychologically when using credit card for a purchase instead of cash. The reason for that is that we don't have a connection of paying for the product we purchased at that time we charge our credit card. A discipline that you may try for the next 30 days is to pay with cash instead of using a credit card when purchasing items at the store or a restaurant. This exercise should open your eyes to how easy it can be for us to just pull out the credit card and charge something. A credit card can be just too easy to use at times and not much thought is given to paying for the actual purchases when the credit card bill comes in.

If you start to pay with cash out of your pocket the spending can seem more real to you and you will also realize how fast you can spend your money if not giving careful thought and consideration prior to purchases.

There are certain benefits to using a credit card that I will certainly acknowledge. It is nice having the convenience of a credit card not having to find cash and change with every purchase and it can be nice to make one big payment at the end of the month as well. Most bank credit card companies these days offer some type of rewards program; flight miles, cash back, or other points toward products. If you are disciplined with your credit card you should take advantage of these rewards programs as they are essentially a discount for you on the money you are spending. Just be careful to not fall into the trap of trying to save by spending more.

100 *Stop the Shop Therapy.*

Don't shop to make yourself feel better. We all have challenges from time to time and problems that need to be addressed. Shopping to cure your ills is like eating comfort foods when you don't feel well. These are both short-term solutions that can create long-term problems for you. The short-term tactic of trying to make yourself feel better may potentially create debt for you that you do not want and need, and in the case of eating you may put on weight that you later regret.

Shopping for emotional support is not a good habit to get into as every time you have a rough day you may end up with an expensive habit rewarding yourself by spending money you don't have or did not intend to spend. Be honest with yourself prior to spending the money, and ask yourself if you are just trying to cover up a bad feeling.

Find inexpensive things to do when not in a good mood other than shopping. One of the best things you can do for yourself is to get some exercise. Just going out for a walk in the fresh air is one of the most uplifting and refreshing things we can do. Talk with a friend as well which can be a great sounding board and better yet volunteer and serve someone else; it will be rewarding and you are most likely to realize your problems are not that big.

101 *Reward yourself and share*

"The best investment with the least risk and the greatest dividend is giving"

- Sir John Templeton, Investor and Philanthropist

When you have accumulated the wealth that you set out to create years prior, you will be a terrific sense of accomplishment. It may now sound strange after all the previous principles to say that it is ok to spend some of your money as a reward but that is what you should do after you have been successful on the road to your goal. You should certainly apply all the prior principles and actions in your spending. When you are hitting your targets you should feel the reward with your investments but also in spending some for yourself on things that you really want or perhaps taking a trip you have wanted to take. You may have learned by now that some of your most treasured rewards do not cost much money after all. That should be an added bonus to all your efforts.

You should also think ahead about how you will plan to spend some of your wealth prior to having it as this is a great visualization exercise. People with wealth have to consider how they will invest, spend, and pass along their wealth to their heirs. If you don't think ahead about this you may never achieve wealth. Educate your children as well so they do not waste the money that you have worked hard to achieve.

Consider those outside your family that you will want to touch and help also. Giving is one of the most rewarding things we can do for others. Giving can also create ongoing support and encouragement to others doing more than you possibly imagined.

Closing comments.

As you move forward continue to review the principles in this book as they may apply to you in different ways at various times of your life. If you apply them consistently, I have no doubt that you will achieve your goals. I wish you the best success on your road to wealth!

For more visit,
www.101PrinciplestoWealth.com

ABOUT THE AUTHOR

Charles Brokop is the president & founder of Clear Stream Advisors Corporation, a registered investment advisor. He has over 30 years of investment experience and has developed a proprietary Absolute Return Strategy investment model called the "S.H.A.R.P. Method. ™" Charles has taught Investment Risk-Management, Option Models, and consulted for investment professionals as well as institutional money managers with over $700 million in managed assets worldwide.

Charles is a contributing writer at Seeking Alpha on Index Strategies, was a guest speaker at the Global Indexing & ETF Conference, has appeared as a guest on various radio programs, and holds numerous board-level positions. He holds a business degree from Arizona State University and has graduate studies at Harvard University. Prior to Clear Stream Advisors was responsible for over $100 million in sales at Cisco Systems, while there for 12 years. He resides in Scottsdale, Arizona and is the proud father of his 2 daughters, Lexi and Camryn.

Made in the USA
Monee, IL
04 November 2026

67385476R10095